Three Shakespearean Themed Plays

SHAKESPEARE OVER MY SHOULDER

TRILOGY

Shakespeare Over My Shoulder

The Cause, My Soul
Prequel to Othello

The Tears of Shylock

TED LANGE

The Brown Bard

STRATTON
—PRESS—
Publishing Life

Shakespeare Over My Shoulder Trilogy
Copyright © 2021 **Ted Lange**

Stratton Press Publishing
831 N Tatnall Street Suite M #188,
Wilmington, DE 19801
www.stratton-press.com
1-888-323-7009

ISBN (Paperback): 978-1-64895-438-2
ISBN (Ebook): 978-1-64895-439-9

Printed in the United States of America

Plays Also by Ted Lange

Four Queens, No Trump
George Washington's Boy
Lady Patriot
Lemon Meringue Façade
Let Freedom Ring
Footnote Historian Trilogy: George Washington's Boy
The Journals of Osborne P. Anderson
Lady Patriot

Dedicated to

Those who love Shakespeare

INTRODUCTION

My first introduction to Shakespeare was offered to me in the form of a bribe when I was in ninth grade. Earlier in the year, I had played Ebenezer Scrooge from *A Christmas Carol* and the acclaim and popularity of being a star on a stage with a captive audience was intoxicating to my smart-alecky class clown persona. My English teacher, Mr. Alan Flores, recognized this and also knew that my nemesis, Donald Germany, would be the perfect foil to use as bait. So he dangled the role of Macbeth to me on the condition that my usual wisecracks and humorous quips disrupting the class would be held at bay or Donald would be offered the role. I agreed to be a model student, knowing my proclivity to crack a joke at every turn would be a tongue-biting battle. I was able to keep my lips sealed and my eyes on the future theatrical praise and adoration I would garner for my next foray on the stage. I had no preconceptions of the aura of Shakespeare, so I brought my street-smart black penchants to the stage. Wisely, Mr. Flores changed scenes and cut dialogue to make it accessible for the Golden Gate Junior High School black student body. My final scene with MacDuff was a sword fight, and Mr. Flores moved the famous "Tomorrow and tomorrow and tomorrow" speech as my Macbeth's dying soliloquy. The applause of that role started me on a path to a lifelong affair with the bard. I loved his words!

First Lesson: you don't have to blindly stick to the script. Know your audience. You can edit, rearrange, and move dialogue to engage your spectators.

In eleventh grade, my high school drama teacher, Tom Whayne, used the role of Banquo to lure me into another Shakespearean escapade. Mr. Whayne showed me how integrate the mindset of the sixties into a play from the seventeenth century. Mr. Whayne loved jazz and was into Miles Davis, so he used this to flavor the scenes as background music for the play. Pop Art was also emerging in the sixties, and Mr. Whayne used a Pop Art Artist to design our set. We created a Shakespeare that was "hip."

Second Lesson: if you have a creative concept for the presentation of a Shakespearian play, go for it and find multiple avenues to support your vision.

Upon graduation from high school, I auditioned for and was awarded the part of Romeo in the New Shakespeare Company's production of *Romeo and Juliet*. Margrit Roma, our director, had the idea of presenting Shakespeare traditionally but with a multi-ethnic cast. Romeo was obviously black and Juliet was white. There was no need to debate why the two families were feuding. Friar Lawrence was also black, and it was a wonderful mix of color-blind casting. A memorable moment for me was every time our Hungarian actress with a thick accent delivered the prologue, saying, "Two households both alike in dig-gah-han-ty." This was 1967, and Bay Area, folks were in the heat of police brutality, the creation of the Black Panther Party for Self-Defense, and integration. Establishment newspapers were not ready to review a cutting-edge version of this classic play. Nonetheless, we eventually were reviewed, ran for two years, and I acted with two Juliets.

When I moved to Los Angeles in the early 1970's, not many black actors were performing Shakespeare. Black Theatre was all the rage; however, I found a kindred spirit in Imam J.D. Hall. He was a traditionalist and I was not. During a notable argument about *Midsummer's Night Dream*, he maintained that Puck should be played by a small actor, and I insisted that was nonsense. I contended that Puck could be played just as effectively by a three-hundred-pound actor. The other fairies simply needed to generate a balance and create a viable vision.

Throughout my theatrical years, I have created some wonderful tableaus using Shakespeare's text to explore the human condition and style the bard's words to be more accessible to black audiences. For the Inner City Cultural Center, I directed a production of Hamlet starring Glynn Turman. The music of Elton John's *Funeral for a Friend* opened the play, and Ophelia's funeral was staged as a New Orleans' style funeral complete with a second line. The review of that production is in a book called *Shakespeare in Sable: A History of Black Shakespearean Actors* by Errol Hill. While many white critics didn't relate to it, my target black audiences loved it. Also, at Inner City Cultural Center, I produced and starred in a highly stylized version of *Othello*. Channeling my early high school experiences, I strove to create scenes, music, and dances that would relate, mirror, and engage my audiences with the black experience.

In Oakland, California, at the Oakland Ensemble Theatre, I directed a production of *Richard III* and used music from Neil Diamond's album, *Hot August Night*, the first cut, "Crunchy Granola Suite." The music goes from classic cellos to rock 'n' roll guitar. Just before the first lyric is sung, the music cuts out and Richard, Ron Thompson, does his "Now is the Winter of Our Discontent" speech. Underneath it, Santana's driving guitar is played. Another black audience rave review!

My latest venture was done at the North Carolina Black Theatre Festival in Winston-Salem, North Carolina. I directed a production of *Twelfth Night or What You Will, Mon.* I replaced all the Shakespearean melodies with Bob Marley songs and set the action on the isle of Jamaica. Once again, the audience responded with delight and enthusiasm, mon!

The genius of the Shakespearean works that delighted a young black student in the sixties is their ability to stand the test of time and be relevant to modern times. The virtuosity of Shakespearean universal themes and characters is their ability to transcend cultures and politics and reflect our shared human condition. My classical education of Shakespeare's time-honored words has shaped me from a nerdish teenager into an avid scholar of the bard, and I truly believe that Shakespeare, whomever you wish to attribute his works to, is looking over my shoulder as I act, create, and write.

Shakespeare
Over My
Shoulder

Dedicated to

Tom Whayne,
My High School Drama Teacher

Alan Flores
My Junior High School English Teacher

Shakespeare over My Shoulder was performed as a Zoom reading at noon was on April 11, 2020.

EDWARD DE VERE	Gordon Goodman
WILLIAM SHAKSPERE (SHAKESPEARE)	Daniel Barrett
CHRISTOPHERE MARLOWE	Steve Ducey
SIR FRANCIS BACON	Stephen Spiegel
NARRATOR	Mary Lange

Shakespeare over My Shoulder was performed again as a Zoom reading at noon on April 18, 2020. This performance was recorded and is available on YouTube.

EDWARD DE VERE	Gordon Goodman
WILLIAM SHAKSPERE (SHAKESPEARE)	Daniel Barrett
CHRISTOPHERE MARLOWE	Steve Ducey
SIR FRANCIS BACON	Stephen Spiegel
NARRATOR	Mary Lange

AUTHOR'S NOTES

The seed for *Shakespeare over My Shoulder* was planted in 1967. I joined an acting company called Shakespeare '67 and auditioned for the part of Romeo in an interracial production of *Romeo and Juliet*. Margrit Roma, the director, and her husband, C. L. Rickclefs, the producer, wanted to mount a trail-blazing version of this play in San Francisco and eventually renamed the company The New Shakespeare Company. As soon as I landed the role, I began researching everything I could find about Romeo, Italy, and Shakespeare. To my astonishment, I discovered a theory that claimed that Shakespeare didn't write all of the plays attributed to him. *The Secret Teaching of All Ages* by Many P. Hall stated that there is no doubt that Sir Francis Bacon was the true writer of the Shakespearean plays. I asked Roma about this, and she said, "Learn your lines and focus on who Romeo is." Hmmm…a seed was planted.

In 1984, I was at the Royal Academy of Dramatic Arts in London, studying Shakespeare, of course! I was introduced to a book, *The Mysterious William Shakespeare: The Myth and the Reality* by Charlton Ogburn. This book asserted that Edward De Vere, the seventeenth Earl of Oxford, was the true author of the Shakespearean plays. My teacher, David Perry, refused to comment. Hmmm…the seed started to sprout.

In Los Angeles, I joined The Shakespeare Authorship Roundtable, organized by Carol Sue Lipman. This was a forum for scholars who pitch controversial ideas about the authorship of the Shakespearean plays. The one common thread was that no one believes the plays were the works of just one man from Stratford upon Avon, William Shakespeare. Possible writers included: Torquato Tasso, the Italian poet, as well as some English ladies, and even Queen Elizabeth herself! I also learned that *Othello* is based on an Italian novella, *Hecatonmmithi* by Giovanni Basttista Giraldi, nicknamed Cinthio. While the novella never reached England and there was a French translation, *Othello* bears a closer relationship to the Italian version. Edward DeVere travelled to Italy as a young man and he spoke fluent Italian. Shakespeare never left England. Who was more likely to be the author? All these proposals were backed up by research and seemed both reasonable and plausible. Hmmm…it was starting to rain on my seed.

Next, I attended an Oxfordian conference at the Mark Twain House in Harford, Connecticut. At the conference, I talked about my Shakespearean-inspired play, *The Cause My Soul: A Prequel to Othello.* After my lecture, a number of Oxfordians apprised me about the following books that support Edward DeVere's authorship claims: J Thomas Looney's *Shakespeare Identified*, Bonnie Miller Cutting's *Necessary Mischief,* Katherine Chiljan's *Shakespeare Suppressed*, Eva Turner Clark's *Hidden Allusions in Shakespeare's Plays*, B. M. Ward's *The Seventeenth Earl of Oxford 1550–1604,* and last but not least, Hank Whittemore's *100 Reasons Shakespeare Was the Earl of Oxford.*

Hmmm…the seed was beginning to bud. What if I could write a play about these four characters meeting? What if William Shakespeare, Francis Bacon, Edward DeVere, and Christopher Marlow were all in the same room? Maybe I could take the research and history of each man and weave it into a story about the authorship of the Shakespearean plays. I knew I didn't have enough information on Christopher Marlow. Not yet the right season for my seed to flourish

Coincidentally, when I returned to Los Angeles, I attended another Shakespeare Round Table and Ed Ayres spoke to the group hypothesizing that Christopher Marlow was actually Shakespeare. Ed and his brother, Alex, wrote a book, *Ghost Writer*, not yet published at that time, which compiled the research supporting the Marlowe assertation. He offered to send copies of the book through email, and I immediately signed up. Hmm…time to fertilize my seed.

Shortly after that, I was at Ohio State University directing a student production of *Red Velvet* by Lolita Chakrabarti. This play is the story of Ira Aldridge, the black American Shakespearean actor, in nineteenth century London. Immersed in all things Shakespeare, *Shakespeare over My Shoulder* started to emerge. I wrote in the daytime and directed in the evening. As always when I begin writing, elements started to nourish my garden. I told my friend, Fred Grandy, Gopher from *Love Boat*, about my concept and he suggested I read *Contested Will* by James Shapiro. At Ohio State, I had entry to one of the finest libraries in the country and Beth Kattleman, associate professor and curator of the Jerome Lawrence and Robert E. Lee Theatre Research Institute, granted me access to many wonderful resources surrounding Marlowe. Cross referencing is a mainstay of my writing. My seed was blooming…

In March 2020, when Covid-19 quarantined America, I also learned that there was a pandemic in London in 1593. I was isolated at home and could relate to the environment I was creating for *Shakespeare over My Shoulder*. The season for this seed had finally come to flourish. I finished the play but was disappointed that I wouldn't be able to do a table read to hear how it sounds…my usual process after completing a play. My wife, Mary, suggested a Zoom reading and the rest is Covid-19 history. I enlisted some of my favorite actors from Los Angeles and New York and invited audiences to listen and watch. After the readings, I pruned and weeded this project to fruition. Based on my discoveries over multiple decades combined with a little comedic artistic license, *Shakespeare over My Shoulder* is my theatrical garden of the probable roles these four men played in the Shakespearean authorship plot.

SYNOPSIS

This mystery remain'd undiscover'd. But 'tis all one to me for had I been the finder-out of this secret, it would not have relish'd among my other discredits.

—William Shakespeare

For four hundred years, scholars have debated this mystery and searched for the truth: who really wrote the Shakespearean plays? Some researchers believe that Christopher Marlowe was the sole playwright, while others propose that it is Edward De Vere, the seventeenth Earl of Oxford. Still many English academics insist that Sir Francis Bacon, one of the great literary minds of Queen Elizabeth's court, wrote the plays. And of course, there are also the intransigent Shakespearean intellectuals who vehemently contest that the plays are the works of just one man from Stratford upon Avon, William Shakspere.

Shakespeare Over My Shoulder ponders this mystery with the four likely contenders at center stage. They reconnoiter at the Mermaid Tavern in 1593, as the bubonic plaque rages through London. It is a pandemic and all the theatres have been closed. As playwrights, they muse their futures with practicality and comedy and lend an ear to the Shakespearean conundrum.

"If we shadows have offended,
Think but this, and all is mended,
That you have but slumb'red here
While these visions did appear."

DRAMATIS PERSONAE

Edward De Vere, forty-five years old, is a poet and playwright.
William Shakspere (Shakespeare), twenty-nine years old, is an actor from Stratford upon Avon.
Christopher Marlowe, twenty-nine years old, is a playwright and spy.
Sir Francis Bacon, thirty-three years old, is a poet and playwright.

ACT I

Scene 1

Scene opens in London's Mermaid Tavern. May 1, 1593. The Earl of OXFORD is writing. SHAKSPERE enters, he is wearing a long scarf which works as a mask, covering his mouth and nose. The scarf is to protect against the plague. Shakspere watches Oxford, looking over his shoulder for a moment.

OXFORD

Why are you standing there?

SHAKSPERE

I'm just looking over your shoulder. What are you writing?

OXFORD

A poem.

Shakspere sits across from him and takes off his scarf.

SHAKSPERE

No, no, no. A poem? Do you have a new a play? I need a play.

OXFORD

Shouldn't we keep our social distance?

SHAKSPERE

You look healthy. We're good. After the plague, when the theatres re-open, I do not want to scrounge for work. Are you working on any new plays?

OXFORD

This plague is giving us a little time to hone our work. I have scribbled a few notes, and I've got an idea that I think has promise.

SHAKSPERE

Is there a role for me? My money is low. Oxford, I want to do one of your plays.

OXFORD

Too soon to tell. Still developing it.

SHAKSPERE

What have you got so far? Tell me. I bet I can play a role. I'm good enough to tear a part to passions.

OXFORD

Shakspere, I heard thee speak me a speech once…but it was not acted.

SHAKSPERE

Was it lofty? I am known to make my speeches lofty.

OXFORD

I think you saw the air too much…thus.

Oxford waves his hands.

SHAKSPERE

Not I. For certainty, I speak my words trippingly on my tongue!

OXFORD

I think you a robustious peri-wig pated fellow, friend Shakspere. I've seen you tear a passion to tatters, to very rags.

SHAKSPERE

Not with good writing. You Oxford are a wonderful writer. I saw Marlowe's *Tamburlaine*, not as good as <u>your</u> writing.

OXFORD

I helped with him with that.

SHAKSPERE

I could tell…that is when his verse started to sing. I would do your words wonderful justice.

OXFORD

Why are you out and about? Shouldn't you be home?

SHAKSPERE

I've cleaned my room three times in five days. Sitting in a room watching the same four walls can drive a man crazy. I re-arranged my furniture twice. And every time I looked out my window, empty streets. I need people.

OXFORD

Not a good thing to need during a plague.

SHAKSPERE

I keep my distance. I will also need a job when this plague has ended. Friend Oxford, I'm really good at soliloquies.

OXFORD

You…suit the action to the word? The word to the action?

SHAKSPERE

An unrelenting yes. A hundred times yes. No, a thousand times yes. I say opportunity is the essential gift to any thespian…but as hard to find as an agate stone. What is this new play you write?

OXFORD

A comedy. Centered on twins.

SHAKSPERE

My chief humor is to play a tragedy, yet I could do a comedy. I can squeeze a laugh and peel a joke. I like the sound of laughter wafting up from the groundlings. Yes, this I might do well, if you cast me in your play. Which twin would I play?

OXFORD

Shakspere I haven't assigned you a role.

SHAKSPERE

Who are the twins?

OXFORD

I am adapting Plautus. Not just one set of twins, but two sets of twins.

SHAKSPERE

Excellent idea.

OXFORD

You'll say anything to get a part.

SHAKSPERE

True. But this does not mean I'm not a good actor. I recognize talent. You recognize talent. I can find another actor that looks like me.

OXFORD

One set of twins is named Antipholus of Ephesus and Antipholus of Syracuse. To contrast their servants Dromio of Ephesus and Dromio of Syracuse.

SHAKSPERE

Farce. I'm laughing already. Let me play Dromio.

OXFORD

Of Ephesus or of Syracuse?

SHAKSPERE

(Takes a beat.) You choose.

OXFORD

No. I have an actor in mind. But maybe you could play *Pinch*.

SHAKSPERE

What is *Pinch*? A lover or a tyrant?

OXFORD

A schoolmaster.

SHAKSPERE

Worthy role for an educated actor.

OXFORD

So you say. Can you act literate?

SHAKSPERE

Let me audition for you. I've got a speech I've written. It's a soldier's soliloquy.

OXFORD

Let me hear it.

SHAKSPERE

Now is the winter of our discontent
made glorious summer by this son of York;

And all the clouds that low'r'd upon our house
In the deep bosom of the ocean buried.

OXFORD

Hold it, hold it, hold it. Stand up, go over there, and do it.

Shakspere gets up from the table and walks away a few paces. He hunches over like Richard III and limps when he walks.

OXFORD

Are you trying to ridicule my walk?

SHAKSPERE

No. I'm doing Richard the Third.

OXFORD

Ah, I see! You look like Robert Cecil. Continue.

SHAKSPERE

Now are our brows bound with victorious wreathes
Our bruised arms hung up for monuments,
Our stern alarums changed to merry meetings
Our dreadful marches to delightful measures
Grim visag'd war hath smooth'd his wrinkled front;
And now, instead of mounting barbed steeds
To fright the souls of fearful adversaries,
He capers nimbly in a lady's chamber
To the lascivious pleasing of a lute.

OXFORD

Bend over a little more. Make it look more like you have a hunchback.

Shakspere hunches over a little more.

SHAKSPERE

But I that am not shap'd for sportive tricks
Nor made to court an amorous looking-glass;
I that am rudely stamp'd and want love's majesty
To strut before a wanton ambling nymph;
I, that am curtail'd of this fair proportion
Cheated of feature by dissembling nature
Deform'd, unfinish'd, sent before my time
Into this breathing world scarce half made up,
And that dogs bark at me as I halt by them…

OXFORD (laughs)

Ha! One hundred percent Robert Cecil.

SHAKSPERE

Why, I, in this weak piping time of peace,
Have no delight to pass away the time,
Unless to see my own shadow in the sun
and descant on mine own deformity,
And therefore, since I cannot prove a lover
To entertain these fair well-spoken days
I am determined to prove a villain.

OXFORD

Hold it, hold it, hold it. I want you to do something else. Something
that has some lyricism to it. Here…read my poem.

SHAKSPERE

You did like what I just did, right?

OXFORD

Just read this…"Venus and Adonis."

SHAKSPERE

Certainly, but who is my character?

OXFORD

Anyone you want. You are reading to get the next job. Got it?

SHAKSPERE

Got it.
Even as the sun with purple-color'd face
Had ta'en his last leave of the weeping morn.
Rose-cheek'd Adonis hied him to the chases
Hunting he love'd but love he laugh'd to scorn
Sick-thoughted Venus makes a main unto him
And like a bold fac'd suitor gins to woo him.

OXFORD

Stop, Shakspere. Please stop.

Oxford moves his chair and turns so his back is facing Shakspere.

OXFORD

Now continue…

SHAKSPERE

But you can't see me.

OXFORD

Young Shakspere, acting is not the art of making faces. It's the art of investing emotion into words and thoughts. Stand over my shoulder…here. And let me listen to you handle verse. Let me hear you act the words. Let me hear the poetry and the emotion of what you are saying.

SHAKSPERE

"Thrice fairer than myself" thus she began

"The field's chief flower, sweet above compare
Stain to all Nymphs, more lovely than a man
More white and red than doves and roses are
Nature, that made thee with herself at strife
Saith that the world hath ending with thy life."

OXFORD

Better…much better.

SHAKSPERE

Do I get the part?

OXFORD

Too soon to tell. Let's leave that open…for the moment.

SHAKSPERE

Oxford, can I show you something? It's a letter from home.

Shakspere hands a worn letter to Oxford.

OXFORD

Good news? Or bad news?

SHAKSPERE

My son is sick. Damn my wife.

Oxford continues to read the letter.

OXFORD

Where do they live?

SHAKSPERE

Oxford, I'm from a place called, Stratford-upon-Avon. Small town. A hamlet really. I left when I was twenty-one. Just headed out looking for fame, fortune, and new adventures.

OXFORD

Every young man's dream. When I was that age, I was travelling Europe.

SHAKSPERE

The trick is not to have children before you realize what you want to do.

OXFORD

What do you have? Boys? Girls?

SHAKSPERE

I've got a daughter, Susanna, and a set of twins. A boy and a girl. Hamnet and Judith. Sweetest children ever.

OXFORD

Miss them?

SHAKSPERE

Let's just say their mother makes it hard for me to return, as often as I would like. You're a noble man...so you don't have to deal with a shrew.

OXFORD

An evil woman does not know class distinction. A sour woman is not class specific. Any man can latch on to the wrong woman at any time. I went looking for adventure as a young man to France and Italy. As I travelled abroad, I was sent word that my new wife was pregnant.

SHAKSPERE

You were ecstatic

OXFORD

Till I did the math.

SHAKSPERE

Oxford, I'm seventeen years old and I had never seen a woman's naked breast. She was twenty-five and willing to let me touch her breast in the bright light of the sun. Not the soft shadowy candle-light of the night. But free as you please, in the daylight, and then she would let me watch those lovely pink nipples rise. Seventeen years old! What should I do? I couldn't wait to bury my passion in her treasure. My god, Oxford, the feeling of my first orgasm at seventeen! She was not a virgin, nor did I care. I just knew the feeling I was experiencing made everyday life special. She led me to an unknown land, and I was happy to be there...but she was twenty-five...I was seventeen. Do you think she took advantage of the situation? It is not till after you are married that you replay the scenario in your head, then you realize that maybe...just maybe... an older woman knows how to manipulate a young boy. Not long after our vows, my daughter Susanna arrived.

OXFORD

What's your wife's name?

SHAKSPERE

Anne.

OXFORD

My wife's name is Anne.

SHAKSPERE

Is your Anne a bitch?

OXFORD

Most decidedly.

SHAKSPERE

Do you think being a bitch is peculiar to women named Anne?

OXFORD

Not in the least. My mistress is also named Anne.

SHAKSPERE

That's a hell of a coincidence.

OXFORD

I suggest to you, Shakspeare…if you must have a mistress make sure she has the same name as your wife. Less complications remembering who you are with.

SHAKSPERE

Anne Hathaway is not the only Anne I have loved.

OXFORD

Meaning?

SHAKSPERE

Oxford, I'll tell you a secret none of my friends know. The Anne I married was not the Anne I loved. There was a young girl, my age, named Anne Whateley…of Temple Grafton. God, she was beautiful! And she loved me…with a true heart and a perfect smile.

OXFORD

Why didn't you marry her?

SHAKSPERE

I tried. I got the marriage license on November 27 from the Bishop of Worcester diocese to marry the woman of my dreams. Anne Whateley loved me…but, Oxford, when sorrows come, they come not single spies, but in battalions. Virgin that she was, and God forgive me, taking that maidenhead was upper most in my mind.

OXFORD

And?

SHAKSPERE

And…I told Hathaway I was going to marry… and it wasn't going to be her.

OXFORD

How did she stop you?

SHAKSPERE

I did the math. She was three months pregnant with Susanna.

OXFORD

Weren't you underage?

SHAKSPERE

Of course, I was! But when your good name is going to be sullied with scandal, a young man's father can use his influence to guarantee certain events proceed in a face-saving manner. The next day, a bond of marriage was made for me…to Anne Hathaway. For what is wedlock forced, but hell. A bit rushed, but very legal.

OXFORD

The good news is you know you are the father of your children. Every time I look into Elizabeth's face, I see the face of her father. I have to believe the stars above us govern our conditions.

SHAKSPERE

But you are a gentleman, an Earl. The Earl of Oxford. You have money and position. You can do what you want. I am ruled by the lack of money. Before the marriage, my dreams were important… after the wedding…all I was told? "You now have a family…you can't do that…" That fustilarian crushed every idea or dream I had and replaced it with the word "obligation." I believe most wives are lesbians.

OXFORD

You do?

SHAKSPERE

Why else would they try to turn their husband into a pussy? I was caught in a bear trap. I needed to find a way out without chewing off my leg. If I stayed, she would crush my spirit.

OXFORD

How did you escape?

SHAKSPERE

When I turned twenty-one, that was the magical year. I poached a deer from the estate of Thomas Lucy. Then before I could be brought to trial, I convinced Anne I had to leave. I left home, hearth, and heartache.

OXFORD

You came to London.

SHAKSPERE

To seek my fortune in the big city. I did not want to be a big fish in a little pond. I wanted to swim with the strong fish and test my mettle. She told me many times: I would never make anything of myself. I was not man enough to deal with the real world. Mark my words, "You'll come running home to the comfort of my arms." I was a princox with wild fantasies.

OXFORD

But you didn't return. I know it wasn't easy. Why did you stick it out here?

SHAKSPERE

Two years after I left, I was so low, I did not know where I would sleep or where my next meal would come from…but I was determined not to prove her right. Sometimes, I think you need someone who doesn't believe in you to give you the strength to keep fighting.

OXFORD

You survived.

SHAKSPERE

I'd rather hold horses in front of a London theatre for one night... than be High Bailiff for a year in Stratford-upon-Avon...and now I am desperate once again. I've got to make money. I need an acting job. Or a job as your valet. What do you require? I'll do anything in the theatre. I can't go home a failure.

OXFORD

Shakspere, I have nothing. Come to me after this plague is over. Maybe I can find something for you to do...it won't be fancy, it may be some menial task. I will keep my eyes and ears open for you.

SHAKSPERE

I would be most grateful. Loan me a shilling for a drink. My parched throat cries out for beer.

Oxford gives him a shilling.

SHAKSPERE

I meant to say give me a shilling. Thanks.

Shakspere wraps his scarf around his mouth and goes to the bar. Oxford continues writing. Christopher MARLOWE enters. He is wearing a long scarf which covers his mouth and nose. He looks around and sits at the table with Oxford.

MARLOWE

Oxford, what are you doing out?

OXFORD

Working on a new poem. I needed exercise and a change of scenery. Luckily, this is one of the few taverns open.

Marlowe takes off his scarf.

MARLOWE

I hate these scarves. Mask your face in the streets or receive a fine. This plague is a pain in my arse. Oxford, I'm working on a new play…but with the plague shutting down 'The Cock-Pit,' I think I need a gimmick to bring audiences back to the theatre.

OXFORD

What's the play?

MARLOWE

I'm calling it *The Jew of Malta*.

OXFORD

What is this fascination that you have with Jews?

MARLOWE

I don't think it's a fascination. They just make great characters in telling a story.

OXFORD

Oh, great characters? Didn't you write another play with a Jewish character?

MARLOWE

I haven't finished that play yet. I am going to produce this play first. Maybe later I may produce the Shylock character in another play. Right now, I am fleshing out this Jew, Barabas. I am using him as the main character for this play. It is so easy to draw conflict through the Jewish lifestyle.

OXFORD

I don't need a Jew to draw conflict for my plays.

MARLOWE

Oxford, the great thing about using Jews is no one in England has seen them since 1299. There is no point of reference. So I can write whatever I want.

OXFORD

I've seen a Jew…as recently as last week.

MARLOWE

No, you haven't.

OXFORD

Yes, I have. There are Jews living here secretly.

MARLOWE

How do you know the person you saw was a Jew?

OXFORD

I felt the horns on his head.

MARLOWE

Proves nothing.

OXFORD

Marranos is what they call themselves. A Jew will tell you he's a Jew…if he trusts you.

MARLOWE

You're trustworthy?

OXFORD

And I can keep a secret.

MARLOWE

The only secret you can keep is a truth you don't know.

OXFORD

I know your benefactor.

MARLOWE

The Queen?

OXFORD

Her too...but I'm speaking of Roger Manwood. Deny it.

MARLOWE

Mr. Manwood? How do you know he is my benefactor?

OXFORD

When you went to court for killing someone in a street brawl. What was your punishment?

MARLOWE

Oxford, you are black.

OXFORD

I'm what?

MARLOWE

You are black. I am black. You are the kettle and I am the pot.

OXFORD

Ah, yes...the kettle calling the pot...black.

MARLOWE

Exactly. Where did you quarrel with Phillip Sidney?

OXFORD

On a tennis court in White Hall.

MARLOWE

Ah, yes. The tennis court fight.

OXFORD

It was a minor argument, and it was resolved.

MARLOWE

And how did you get that limp you try to compensate for?

OXFORD

Everyone knows I got it in a street fight.

MARLOWE

An argument with Sir Thomas Knyvet?

OXFORD

That too has been resolved…and I have the wound in my leg to prove it.

MARLOWE

So I think you do not have enough ground to stand on to reprimand me. William Bradley was not killed by me. I was there, but I did not strike the blow that ended his life. Tom Watson and I were minding our own business when Bradley got a notion in his head, he could overpower Tom. Never fight with a swordsman who is better than you. Tom is a master. Bradley drew his sword, I stepped back, and Tom made swift work of defeating his opponent. I think Tom let Bradley wound him, for after he did, Tom pierced him through the heart. Tom's wound helped our case, and the judge saw the injustice of the situation. But I struck no blow to hurt or kill William Bradley.

OXFORD

How subject we young men are to this vice of fighting.

MARLOWE

Let us say that no one knows better than you of this vice. Oxford, I was innocent. And I do not have the favor of the Queen to advocate for me.

OXFORD

No, just a judge. Who better to assist in a courtroom trial than the weight of a judge? Marlowe, the truth can bend. A judge sits on the bench weighs the evidence with his own values, not the law. Who was the judge that sat on the bench for your trial?

MARLOWE

Roger Manwood.

OXFORD

I rest my case. Marlowe, it is a dangerous game you play, and if you continue to play, you may end up dead sooner than later...or with a limp like mine. There will not always be a Manwood to guide circumstances. And remember, the Queen can be manipulated.

MARLOWE

There is artistry to this game...like backgammon...you roll the dice, but those numbers do not determine the end of your game. Strategy determines the outcome. Position, experience and a little luck. Less luck than you might imagine. If you play the game without emotion, you can win.

OXFORD

You are as a candle, the better part burnt out. How many characters in your new play?

MARLOWE

Near twenty.

OXFORD

How many women?

MARLOWE

Got some nuns, an abbess, a daughter, and of course, a courtesan.

OXFORD

Of course. I have a gimmick for you. Innovative yet secure.

MARLOWE

My ears cry out for security.

OXFORD

Let women play the female roles.

MARLOWE (Laughs.)

Oxford! I'm serious and you decide to induce my laughter.

OXFORD

Marlowe, you mistake my tone. I lay at your feet an ingenious idea. What could be more fascinating to see on stage than an actual female attempting to portray her gender? You would be innovative.

MARLOWE

I have obligations to my boys.

OXFORD

This isn't about obligations, it's about art. Think of the controversies your play would generate. First whispers, then passionate talk, then angry debates. Debates would turn into attendance and ultimately guilders in your coffers. The question is…do you want to be in the forefront as a playwright and producer?

MARLOWE

To be or not to be? that is the question. I ask you for a simple suggestion and you give me revolution. I don't need the aggravation.

OXFORD

Someday it'll happen. Someday a woman will share the stage with a man. Be a man ahead of his time, Kit.

Shakspere comes over to the table. He stands behind Marlowe and mouths the words, "Is that Christopher Marlowe?" Oxford nods yes.

MARLOWE

Oxford, is there a fishmonger standing over my shoulder unannounced?

Oxford nods yes. Shakspere comes around the table to face Marlowe.

SHAKSPERE

Excuse me, Christopher Marlowe, right?

MARLOWE

Yes.

Shakspere takes his hand and shakes it enthusiastically.

SHAKSPERE

I am a great admirer of your work. What a fantastic writer you are! I saw your play, *Dido, Queen of Carthage.* The way you handle blank verse is amazing. One speech in it I chiefly loved, t'was Aeneas to Dido.

MARLOWE

Thank you and you are?

SHAKSPERE

Shakspere, William Shakspere. I am an actor.

MARLOWE

A pleasure to meet you, but right now, I am in the middle of an intimate conversation with my friend here, Mr. DeVere.

SHAKSPERE

Yes, we talked earlier. He was kind enough to buy me a drink.

MARLOWE

I see.

SHAKSPERE

I just wanted to say to you, I hope to someday to be in one of your plays. You have such a perceptive eye when it comes to writing character.

MARLOWE

Thank you. If we could get back to our conversation?

SHAKSPERE

Sure. Absolutely. I don't want to be an intruder. Just remember, if you ever need a talented actor, I am available.

MARLOWE

I will keep that in mind.

SHAKSPERE

I know you have an eye for brilliance. An eye and an ear.

MARLOWE

That's a compliment.

SHAKSPERE

I would be happy to audition for you anytime. I can play many varied kinds of roles...romantic, heroic, comedic, or tragic. All I need is a chance. Whatever role is uncast...think of me to fill the void. Be it man or woman, girl or boy. Let the lines cry out for interpretation, then let me seduce the role. If a woman...I can be gentle as a subtle Smilacina flower or as hearty as a buxom chambermaid...or I can play a shrew. I have a particular insight to the characteristics of a shrew.

Shakspere speaks in a woman's angry voice.

SHAKSPERE

"To comb your noodle with a three-legged stool and paint your face and use you like a fool."

MARLOWE

Good to know.

SHAKSPERE

I write. I wrote a soliloquy.

MARLOWE

You did?

OXFORD

Now is the winter of *your* discontent.

SHAKSPERE

Wait! That's my line.

OXFORD

Continue for my friend.

SHAKSPERE

Yes. *Now is the winter of our discontent.* A good start, right?
Now is the winter of our discontent,
made glorious summer by this son of York;
And all the clouds that low'r'd upon our house
In the deep bosom of the ocean buried.

MARLOWE

Hold it, hold it, hold it! Shakspere, this is not a theatre, and today,
I am not auditioning any actors. I just came out to this tavern for
a drink and an uninterrupted conversation with my friend here.
Now I realize this plague has got us all a little batty, but thou dost
infect mine eyes. I can see you are immensely talented, but right
now, I came here to relax...and you are making that unachievable.
Forgive me if I sound a little shrill-tongued.

SHAKSPERE

Certainly, I understand. You are two of England's finest playwrights
and I am just a lowly peasant. I should not intrude. I will just go
over there and play solitaire backgammon.

OXFORD

I hope you win. Thank you! So, Marlowe, what's your thoughts?

Shakspere goes to another part of the tavern. Sits at a table with a backgammon board, his back to the audience. The lights dim on him.

MARLOWE

Would you do it? Would you give a woman a role in one of your plays?

OXFORD

Hell no, but I'm not looking for a gimmick.

MARLOWE

I need a better idea.

OXFORD

You're letting your private parts dictate your art. You shouldn't be involved with any of your young nubile actors. Buggery can be dangerous.

MARLOWE

Politics. It's politics. Simply unavoidable.

OXFORD

Restraint and discipline. Keep your pantaloons up and you avoid politics. Those castrati, you love so well, will be your Achilles heel.

MARLOWE

I can think of a hundred reasons why a woman would be a disaster on stage.

OXFORD

Give me three.

MARLOWE

Pardon me.

OXFORD

Give me three reasons you think a woman on stage would prove a detriment to the execution of one of your plays.

MARLOWE

It's common sense. Simplicity itself. First, they don't have the instrument to articulate their gender. No voice. I need an actor to reach the back row of the 'Cock-Pit Theatre.' Their voice will not have the melodious volume to reach the last seat, in the last row, in the balcony. Words will be lost, consonants will be dropped and vowels will be blurred...and, Oxford, can a woman really understand the poetry of my iambic pentameter? I think not! There is a physical strength that a woman cannot sustain over the core of the

48

evening, the run of the show. A woman is frail, dainty, and inherently weak. How can they stand up to the natural strength of one folksy boy?

OXFORD

I know a lady-in-waiting, strong as a bull.

MARLOWE

There are boys that make better woman than some of the women I know. They have studied, practiced, and perfected the attitudes of a woman. Oxford, I've got to introduce you to some of my lady friends.

OXFORD

I look forward to that day.

MARLOWE

And as delightful as these women are…they cannot touch my boys for femininity.

OXFORD

Maybe I'll decline that invitation.

MARLOWE

Third and most important…a woman does not have the talent to create a full-rounded female emotional depth of character.

OXFORD

Then, if that's true…how can you write her?

MARLOWE

Any woman that likes, enjoys, or wants to be around the theatre is a lady of ill repute. A strumpet that any decent gentleman would shun. Every gentleman knows that, and it will color their character with the reality of their world. The theatre tends to attract trollops and harlots. I would need a woman who can play royalty as well as a wench. Can a harlot play a gentle woman? I think not! I need the audience to get lost in the story, I am trying to tell. Frankly, there aren't any women talented enough to actually play a woman.

OXFORD

Your theory almost works.

MARLOWE

Not a theory, Oxford. Not a theory. A fact.

OXFORD

You better tell the Italians. They've been putting women on the stage for thirty years.

MARLOWE

Be-slubbering, Balderdash!

OXFORD

Did you think the Commedia Dell'Arte was all men? Have you been to Italy?

MARLOWE

Holland and France, my friend. I tend to avoid the South.

OXFORD

Next opportunity…travel South. I suggest Venice.

MARLOWE

Italians…putting a woman on stage. Churlish, pin-butt idiots. Why don't you do it, Oxford?

OXFORD

Young Sophocles, YOU are the up and coming playwright. It falls to your shoulders to carry that weight.

MARLOWE

If I SHOULD do it, you NEED to do it.

OXFORD

No, I must work in the theatre with a hidden hand. It wouldn't be prudent for the Earl of Oxford to innovate the theatre…or draw attention to my involvement…whereas…

MARLOWE

I understand…whereas…I have no such high claims to society. Especially royal society. I'm just the son of a poor shoemaker… and therefore since I am still establishing myself, from my humble beginnings…it falls to me to push the art form forward.

OXFORD

Who better than you to introduce the English audiences to new possibilities?

MARLOWE

You have not put your name on any play that you have written.

OXFORD

True! But certain royal personalities are hearing rumors, and I find myself in a dilemma, if I desire to continue…I must find a mask to cover my face.

MARLOWE

Hurts doesn't it. 'Art' no credit.

OXFORD

Yet…'Art'…just the same.

MARLOWE

The social politics of royalty bear no weight on my achievements. Thank goodness, my father was a shoe repair man.

OXFORD

You are a bright and shining star of London's Theatre. Your verse is magical, structure impeccable, and actors like Edward Allyn seek you out. I see a great future for you, Marlowe…but don't try and sell me the shoe repair man fantasy.

MARLOWE

What are you implying?

OXFORD

You are college educated. What college did you attend?

MARLOWE

Corpus Christi College. Cambridge. Completed my studies in '87.

OXFORD

So are you telling me your father made enough money to send you to college?
Let not the creaking of shoes nor the rustling of silks betray thy poor heart…

MARLOWE

Of course not. I had a benefactor.

OXFORD

May I ask who sponsored you?

MARLOWE

You may ask, but wait not for the answer today.

Francis BACON enters the tavern. He wears a long scarf over his mouth.

BACON

Ahhh, Marlowe. I've been looking for you.

MARLOWE

And fortune smiles on you today.

Bacon takes off his scarf.

BACON

Good to see you, Sir Edward. This scarf is not worth the rude wind
that blows in my face.
Is this blight really in the air and on the streets of London?

OXFORD

Bacon, how much longer do we have to survive this plague?

BACON

Quarantine. When forty days are up. We just have to use caution
and common sense. Marlowe, I've spoken to the Queen. Your life
is in danger.

MARLOWE

Hazards of being the Queen's spy.

BACON

There is a plot brewing against you. You must beware the Privy
Council. The Queen has asked for me to assist in helping with your
rescue. I want you to join my Rosicrucians.

MARLOWE

And what do they do? Write poetry?

BACON

No. We must devise a romantic death for you. The Rosicrucians
will guide you to a safe destination.

OXFORD

Marlowe, you haven't heard of the Secret Order of the Rosey Cross?

MARLOWE

If it's a secret order, I would say no. Who can keep up with all of the secrets that abound in the royal court? Druids, Marranos, and Knights Templar. It's a jungle out there.

OXFORD

"What FATES impose that men must needs abide; It boots not to resist both wind and tide."
Marlowe, it's time for you to die.

MARLOWE

Clever and poetic. But I'm not doing it. I'm not going to disappear, just because London gets a little hot in the spring. I like the tropics; I can handle the situation.

BACON

The Privy Council is plotting your demise. Robert Cecil wants you dead.

MARLOWE

Bacon, I'm in the middle of a very profitable career. I am the brightest star in the firmament. My plays are quite popular. I am even thinking of putting women on the stage. I want to innovate the theatre. I have not reached my prime, and you want to cut me off?

BACON

It's not me. It's the crown. It's the Queen. Do you really want to end up dead? If you let me, we can fake your death. You have made some very powerful people angry. There are deep plots and delicate strategems practiced against you. They're not imaginary. Tis real, but your death doesn't have to be.

MARLOWE

Blank verse. My reasons lie in the written word. Blank verse. I'm getting quite good at it. I used to hate writing, now I can't wait to put pen to paper.

BACON

I understand your passion. I write too.

OXFORD

Men are sometime masters of their fates. Marlowe, I'm sure Bacon would not be insisting if it were not serious.

MARLOWE

No. You don't understand. You think you understand. I've got a trunk full of plays. Blank verse. I'm creating an art form. Who else is doing this?

OXFORD

Me. I'm doing it.

MARLOWE

Not as good as I am doing it…and you don't put your name on any of your plays.

OXFORD

I will give you credit for writing some wonderful words…but you are not the only star in the heavens.

MARLOWE

Oxford, I can write you under this table.

OXFORD

You think you can. Blank verse is not your private toy. Once it becomes popular…think you other writers will not be able to master it? Marlowe, pick your poison and move to the back of the line.

MARLOWE

Oxford, I have had great success with my plays...

OXFORD

Dido, Queen of Carthage, and what? *Massacre at Paris*...Notable but not the huge successes you claim.

MARLOWE

Dido was my first play, and I was just getting my footing. And *Massacre in Paris* was a little too controversial for the Queen. But I am learning the politics of writing. *Tamburlaine the Great, Edward the Second.* Vastly different subject matter, handled by a master. Big successes, deny it?

BACON

You will not witness anything if Robert Cecil, the future Lord Burghley, has his way. He wants your head.

OXFORD

It's the boy, isn't it.

MARLOWE

What boy?

OXFORD

The boy in your troupe. You don't want to leave the boy. Your passion will get you killed.

MARLOWE

You're on the wrong road, in the wrong city, at the wrong time. I am a genius and the general public is starting to acknowledge it. I am gaining a reputation...and I like how it feels.

OXFORD

Stubborn little sodomite, isn't he?

MARLOWE

You're spitting in the wind, Oxford. And who is that Italian boy that cooks for you and lives in your home? Whose bed does he sleep in?

OXFORD

Ah, yes. Once again, the pot calls the kettle black.

BACON

Fame is a dangerous mistress, Marlowe. It is a cannibal that eats your soul. She takes the best part of your talent and inflates your mind with self-importance.

OXFORD

Genius?

MARLOWE

Sir Francis, name another playwright that writes as well as me. Ben Johnson? Not even close. I am not bragging. I am looking at the cold hard facts of talent. Right now, London Theatre is at a turning point. Someone has to lead the pack. Someone has to set the tone and make the rules for what constitutes good play writing. I have discovered I am very good at blank verse. This is an art form just now emerging. Give the devil his due and give me my accolades.

BACON

You fall into the abyss of overconfidence. She makes you think you are stronger than you actually are. She fills your dreams with gold…magnifies your mirror with images of overwhelming power. Be careful, Marlowe…even mature men have been kissed by fame and lost their mind in the scent of her perfume. Fame will suck all of the idealism out of your brain. Protect your talent. Taste the moment…but don't build on its foundation. Secure your future, so that the world will enjoy your talent. Don't let that cunt, Fame, trick you. She's satanic and hungry and wants to control your future. Defy her. She will infect your friends and your family, make them feel you owe them. They will demand their fair share of your spoils. You won't change, but they will. Oh, yes, Marlowe, you think you can handle that bitch...but believe me, I've seen how she can devastate a man's soul and well-being and warp his mind. Take the offer.

MARLOWE

I am my own man, Bacon.

BACON

You must die. The question is where do you want your phoenix to rise?

MARLOWE

I promised Edward Alleyn my new play.

BACON

And we will make sure that he gets it.

MARLOWE

You don't understand...I want to see him act in it.

BACON

You don't understand...you won't be alive to see him act in anything. If you follow my plan, you'll live to write another play. If you don't...all plays die with you. Where do you want to rise again?

Marlowe puts on his mask, then gets up.

MARLOWE

I have to think about this. You are asking a lot of a man who just came out to break the boredom of the plague and have a drink. Maybe play a game of backgammon.
Before I give up this life I love so much...I must walk it out and think on it.

He leaves with a flourish.

BACON

Youth…all swagger, very little substance. What are you writing?

OXFORD

A poem.

BACON

What's it called?

OXFORD

Venus and Adonis.

BACON

May I see it?

Oxford hands Bacon a few pages. Bacon reads it. Oxford stands and paces as Bacon reads. Shakspere comes over to Francis Bacon. He stands behind Bacon's chair and mouths the words "Francis Bacon." Oxford nods yes. Shakspere tries to read what Bacon is reading.

BACON

Oxford, is there a miscreant at my shoulder?

SHAKSPERE

Excuse me, aren't you Francis Bacon?

OXFORD

Oh, oh.

BACON

Why yes…yes, I am.

SHAKSPERE

You write plays, don't you?

BACON

On occasion, I have been known to put pen to paper and scribble out a few choice pieces.

SHAKSPERE

I am an actor.

OXFORD

Would you like to see his audition piece?

BACON

Not particularly.

SHAKSPERE

I wrote a soliloquy.

OXFORD

"Discontent, is following you wherever you go."

SHAKSPERE

If you got something that works, why change it?

OXFORD

I'm starting to feel my discontent.

SHAKSPERE

Sir Francis, my name is Shakspere, William Shakspere. I'm an actor in search of a good play.

BACON

And I am a writer in search of a good idea.

SHAKSPERE

If you ever need an actor, I am the thespian for you. I can act. I do tragical or comical or both at the same time. I do prose, blank verse, and I can memorize a scene faster than an Irishman can tell a lie. I can stage fight scenes, I know how to handle broadsword, rapier, or foil.

Shakspere picks up a broom and takes a swordsman stance and does his sword-fighting moves.

SHAKSPERE

Good? See my form and my execution?

BACON

Every inch King Arthur.

SHAKSPERE

If you wrote a play about say…Henry V, I could stage your battle scenes.
I am an all-around utility actor. Tell me what you need and I can see that it gets done.

BACON

Mr. Shakspere, I will keep all what of you have said in mind, but right now, I am in the middle of a critique with my friend Mr. DeVere.

SHAKSPERE

Oh, yes! Sorry to have bothered you. Just leave word here, in this tavern, when you are auditioning for your next play, and I will be sure to get it. Don't wait till "Saint Crispin's Day."

BACON

I will remember.

Shakspere goes to another part of the Tavern. Bacon holds up his pages to Oxford.

BACON

Oxford, you're not going to publish this, are you?

OXFORD

I was thinking…maybe I should.

BACON

No. No you can't…surely, you're not seriously going to let the general public in on this? Didn't the Queen in arrest you in '80 for treason? She thought you were a Catholic.

OXFORD

We're past that. I'm back in her good graces. We were also once lovers.

BACON

De Vere in this poem "Venus" is she not the Queen?

OXFORD

Of course, yes, she is.

BACON

The Queen will read this, and you will be reprimanded.

OXFORD

Her majesty is making a fool of herself, chasing that young boy in court.

BACON

But you write:
"Look how a bird lies tangled in a net,
So fast'ned in her arms Adonis lies;

Pure shame and aw'd resistance made him fret,
Which bred more beauty in his angry eyes."
Oxford, no, no, no, no, no. Don't do this…and what is this couplet?
"Rain added to a river that is rank
Perforce will force it overflow the bank."
Publish this and the Queen will separate your head from your shoulders.

OXFORD

Bacon, he has no interest in her. Yet she flaunts her power before him.

BACON

Of course, she does. She is the Queen. True, the court knows all this. But others will read this, and it will go wrong for you. How could you write this?

"Still she entreats, and prettily entreats,
For to a pretty car she tunes her tale.
Still is he sullen, still he low'rs and frets
'Twixt crimson shame and anger ashy -pale."
I must say, beautiful and elegant.

OXFORD

Thank you.

BACON

But outrageous…and dangerous, your couplet doesn't help the situation.
"Being red, she loves him best, and being white,
Her best is better'd with a more delight."

OXFORD

She won't be mad. The general public won't know of whom I speak.

BACON

Well, here you are at your subtle best.
"By this the love-sick QUEEN began to sweat,"
You don't find that a bit too obvious? The love-sick Queen?

OXFORD

Finish the line, there's beauty there.

BACON

"For where they lay the shadow had forshook them,
And Titan, tired in the midday heat,
with the burning eye did hotly overlook them,"

OXFORD

The Burning Eye! I love that…don't you love that? Now read the couplet…

BACON

"Wishing Adonis had his team to guide,
So he were like him, and by Venus side."
Every noble man that walks through the royal court will know what you are saying.
This is shameful, Oxford. Listen, just listen to me, you write here…
"And now Adonis, with a lazy sprite,
And with a heavy, dark, dislikening eye,
His low'ring brows o'erwhelming his fair sight,
Like misty vapors when they blot the sky,
Souring his cheeks, cries, **'Fie, no more of love!'"**
Oxford, we were all there for that moment. You will spike her anger with this poem.
"Fie no more of love!" It won't take a genius to know that you have criticized the Queen.
You need a beard. Someone who is not of the court. Someone when asked can say, "I just wrote a poem. I took Ovid's work and turned it into my own." Publish this, and you'll be out of her good graces.

OXFORD

She is being misguided by her advisors.

BACON

Agreed. But, Oxford, you can get a message to her. However, not this way. If she finds out who from her Royal Court is publishing poems about private royal court flirtations and affairs, you will be labeled a traitor and you could lose your head. Or worse, drawn and quartered.

OXFORD

But she has to know. How else can I get her to listen without Lord Burghley whispering in her ear?

BACON

DeVere, you need a beard. Actually, WE need a façade. I have some plays I want to publish. I have said some things that should not be linked to me. Your poem "Venus and Adonis," if this comes from you, you risk losing any royal position you've gained and maybe your life. Retribution will come back, swift to you and your family. Think of your daughter?

OXFORD

Not MY daughter, my wife's daughter. I'm trying to be a bigger man…but when I look in her face, I don't see her mother or me. It's hard, I want to be a mean son of a bitch. I want revenge.

BACON

Didn't you get revenge with your affair to Lady Ann Vavasour?

OXFORD

No. I got a wound to my leg from her brother, Thomas, which gives me this unsightly limp.

BACON

Oxford, we need to find someone not too bright. Someone who loves the theatre and the prospect of being a writer. A man we can pay and manipulate, shower with praise, and he can front our artistic output of literary works.

OXFORD

Maybe someone who is a little desperate for money?

BACON

Exactly. Someone desperate enough to be intimidated by us.

Oxford looks around the room. As Shakspere walks by their table, he calls him over.

OXFORD

Oh, Shakspere! Oh, William Shakspere. Please, come here.

William Shakspere comes over and stands at Oxford's table. He is sipping his drink.

OXFORD

William, we have a proposition for you.

Fast Black Out.

END OF ACT I

ACT II
Scene 1

Mermaid Tavern moments later. Shakspere stands before the seated Oxford and Bacon.

SHAKSPERE

A proposition? What kind of a proposition?

OXFORD

Have a seat. Sir Francis and I want to make a proposal to you.

SHAKSPERE

A role in one of your plays?

Shakspere sits at the table.

OXFORD

Not my plays…your plays.

SHAKSPERE

I am lost. What is the proposition?

OXFORD

You like my writing?

SHAKSPERE

I love your writing.

OXFORD

I write poetry too, but at this moment, I have a dilemma...and I feel only you can help.

SHAKSPERE

Me? More than Sir Francis Bacon?

BACON

Yes. Only you?

SHAKSPERE

But I am not a gentleman...such as yourselves. You all have money, position, titles. I am just a poor thespian looking for a role.

OXFORD

Oh, we have a role for you to play. Quite a unique one.

BACON

The role of a lifetime. Quite literally.

SHAKSPERE

I am most confused gentlemen. Who has written the role? You, Mr. DeVere?

OXFORD

Not I, William.

SHAKSPERE

You, Mr. Bacon?

BACON

No, not I, William.

SHAKSPERE

Then, gentlemen... I am at a total loss for what we are talking about.

BACON

We would like to impose on your good name.

SHAKSPERE

I am waiting for this mystery to conclude. Gentlemen, please arrive at a point so that clarity will issue forth. What are you asking?

OXFORD

How would you like to make a tidy sum?

BACON

Annually.

SHAKSPERE

The answer is yes. Whatever it is?

BACON

William Shakspere. Such a strong forceful name. Simply rolls off the tongue.

OXFORD

We need a front.

BACON

A surrogate. A young fellow traveler such as yourself, at the start of your London theatrical career. Surely, you could use a little guidance.

SHAKSPERE

I am not opposed to advice.

OXFORD

I have written a poem. Which I want to publish. I cannot put my name on it as author…but it must be credited.

BACON

The Earl of Oxford is willing to pay you for the use of your name. We want you to be our front. This may make you famous and hence easier to land roles in new plays.

SHAKSPERE

Famous?

OXFORD

Yes.

SHAKSPERE

But won't you get upset with me if I become famous for the plays you write?

BACON

You alone can suck that tit. I want nothing to do with that bitch… Fame.

OXFORD

Shakspere, as gentlemen, we cannot write our stories and say what we want to say. We want to be free to express our thoughts and ideas and not worry about our social peers getting a sense of where this wind is blowing from.

BACON

We want to camouflage ourselves so that curious minds don't wander back to us…however if we place your name on the bill.

OXFORD

Our friends would wonder how you knew so much about royal situations, and it would leave us free to comment on palace politics and our social order without drawing attention to us.

BACON

See. Simple.

SHAKSPERE

Because I'm a commoner. Royal situations, politics, social order… are you going to libel someone?

OXFORD

Of course not. Feel safe, William.

BACON

We want to send messages to our royal circle of friends…

OXFORD

But we want to remain anonymous. Here is the best part…we will pay you.

BACON

Money for you to put your name on our plays.

OXFORD

Or say an epic poem?

BACON

And if some noble person asks you where you got the idea about a scene or some witty dialogue, your answer will be "I just used my imagination. I am a student of human nature."

SHAKSPERE

I have a good eye for well-written characters. And you will pay me for this?

OXFORD

Handsomely.

BACON

And we will let you put your name on a Kit Marlowe play.

SHAKSPERE

No shit?

OXFORD

I think you could have found a wittier way to express it…but yes.

SHAKSPERE

He won't mind?

BACON

I can honestly say, he will be at a loss of words.

SHAKSPERE

And if Edward DeVere writes a play, you will put my name on it as author?

OXFORD

Yes.

SHAKSPERE

And if you write a play, the name Francis Bacon will be replaced with William Shakspere?

BACON

Light seeking light, doth light of light beguile.

SHAKSPERE

Whatever that means. And you both will pay me for the use of my name. Agreed, I'll be your façade.

BACON/OXFORD

Yes!

SHAKSPERE

Gentlemen. It's a deal.

They shake hands all around to seal the bargain.

BACON

Should we wash our hands?

SHAKSPERE

Why?

BACON

Never mind.

OXFORD

I would like however…to change the spelling of your surname. I would like to add two letters. A and E.

SHAKSPERE (Thinks.)

Shaka-pear?

OXFORD

Shakespeare. Francis, don't you think Shakespeare has a nice ring to it? And it reminds me of the muse Diana, shaking her spear.

BACON

Kind of a poetic touch.

SHAKSPERE

I think we should celebrate, and you should both buy me a drink. I'll get a pitcher of ale.

He gets up and goes to the bar.

OXFORD

A little too eager?

BACON

I hope this doesn't turn around and bite us on the arse.

OXFORD

If we are not careful, this upstart crow is going to actually want to write a play.

Black Out.

Scene 2

Shakspere will be referred to as SHAKESPEARE from this point on.

Shakespeare enters the Mermaid Tavern and sits at a table. He takes out a manuscript from his satchel and lays it in front of him. He is flipping through pages and rereading passages. Edward DeVere enters; he is wearing a long scarf, not as a mask. He limps when he walks. He sits with Shakespeare.

SHAKESPEARE

Eddy! Eddy, we've got to talk.

Oxford takes off his scarf.

OXFORD

Eddy?

SHAKESPEARE

Did you hear about Kit Marlowe? He's dead.

OXFORD

When did this happen?

SHAKESPEARE

Last Wednesday.

OXFORD

How did it happen?

SHAKESPEARE

He was stabbed to death by some bawdy serving man. They were drunk…got into a fight at the widow Eleanor Bull's Tavern…and this guy, Ingram, stabbed Marlowe. Stabbed him! They got into an argument over who was going to pay the bill.

OXFORD

That is terrible. Such a talent wasted. Gone. Such a talent. Gone.

SHAKESPEARE

Yes, that's how I feel. I always wanted to be in one of his plays. Looks like that is never going to happen.

OXFORD

We know he was a bit of a hot head. He could fly off the handle.

SHAKESPEARE

Speaking of talent. I need to talk to you.

OXFORD

Yes?

SHAKESPEARE

Look, I can't let you put my name on this play.

OXFORD

What are you talking about?

SHAKESPEARE

This play is not ready to be produced. It needs another rewrite.

OXFORD

Shakespeare, your job is not to help me write my plays. It's to let me use your name. That's why I pay you. Handsomely I might add.

SHAKESPEARE

Yes, yes, I know. Thank you and I am not ungrateful for the money, but seriously, look at this scene.

OXFORD

What scene?

SHAKESPEARE

Act three, scene four. The scene about the black man's handkerchief. He's really mad with his wife because she can't show him his handkerchief. Her servant Emilia is just standing there, listening... listening to the Black-a-Moor raving mad at his wife. I think we need to rewrite this scene.

OXFORD

We? You're not writing this play, I am. I'm just using your name.

SHAKESPEARE

Yes, Yes, I know...but hear me out. You've got this Othello fellow asking for the handkerchief and his wife Desdemona lies and says she has it. She lies to her husband.

OXFORD

It's part of the plot...the scene has to turn there.

SHAKESPEARE

Yes, but all Emilia has to do is say "I found the handkerchief and gave it to my husband, Iago," but she doesn't. The logic of the scene falls apart. Instead, Emilia is silent. She watches this mad black lunatic raving at his beautiful innocent white wife, and Emilia stays silent. Does that sound logical to you?

OXFORD

Don't worry it will work. Trust me.

SHAKESPEARE

You think the groundlings are going to believe that. You think they're not going to question why? Why doesn't Emilia speak up?

OXFORD

Shakespeare, your job is not to write the plays. I only let you read it as a courtesy, so you can be prepared when others ask you about the plot or characters. Maybe I should stop.

SHAKESPEARE

No. I need to know the plots…but if I don't believe it, how am I going to convince others?

OXFORD

Act.

SHAKESPEARE

Act?

OXFORD

Yes, act. If you are cast as a murderer, are you going to prowl the streets of London looking for someone to kill? No, I don't think so. You are going to ACT like a killer. You said you were a very fine actor. I am now asking you to act like you wrote the plays. Act with great conviction and passion for the words on the page.

SHAKESPEARE

No, no, I understand. But I'm still going to have to ask questions. I have to be on top of the play. Do you really think Englishmen are going to believe a Black Moor is a soldier leading white men? Where did you get this idea anyway?

OXFORD

First of all, he is not just a soldier, he is a general. A famous mercenary. It is quite a famous story in Italy. It is in a novella written by
Giovanni Basttista Giraldi.

SHAKESPEARE

Never heard of him.

OXFORD

"Cinthio?" Of course, you haven't, but that's not important. What
is important is that it is a great story. From a popular Italian novella.

SHAKESPEARE

If it's so popular, how come it didn't come to England?

OXFORD

I'M bringing it to England…in MY play.

SHAKESPEARE

What's the name of this high and mighty Italian novella?

OXFORD

Hecatonmmithi (Heck-ah-to-myth-ee).

SHAKESPEARE

Never heard of it.

OXFORD

Of course, you haven't. Have you ever travelled out of England?

SHAKESPEARE

No.

OXFORD

Do you read Italian?

SHAKESPEARE

No.

OXFORD

Then I think it is safe to say, "You don't know what the hell you're talking about." My suggestion to you, Shakespeare, is that you get a copy of the novella, read it in its Italian, then come back to me with your criticisms. Only then can we talk about changes that need to be made to MY play.

SHAKESPEARE

Yes, yes, I understand. Don't be so sensitive. Mr. Edward DeVere, Mr. Earl of Oxford, Mr. "Can't change a line of my play." But let me ask you one more question...and then I'll be quiet. The speech about the handkerchief, the Egyptian charmer that was a mind reader...is the black general really that superstitious?

OXFORD

Yes.

SHAKESPEARE

All right, all right, all right...I am well aware of black people believing in magic. Black magic, pardon the pun...but does the Italian girl believe in this mumbo jumbo too?

OXFORD

You're missing the point, Shakespeare. And I think you can be forgiven for that with your limited intellectual abilities. I think when you see it on the stage, then and only then will you get a sharper understanding of what is going on dramatically in the play.

SHAKESPEARE

So you like this line, "That handkerchief did an Egyptian to my mother give she was a charmer and could almost read the thoughts of people: she told her, while she kept it, t'would make her amiable and subdue my father entirely to her love." Do you really like that line?

OXFORD

Love it.

SHAKESPEARE

Well, I think you could do better. Just a thought. You might want to think about a rewrite.

OXFORD

Shakespeare, stick to drinking ale and sending money home to your wife. Leave the writing to me and to Bacon. We are poets. You are an actor that was blessed with a great opportunity. Enjoy your moment. In a hundred years, we will all be gone and none of this will matter. Try not to mix your knowledge of poetry with my knowledge of structure, character, and blank verse. We are not equals.

SHAKESPEARE

You're telling me as a playwright you don't want to listen to the thoughts of an actor?

OXFORD

Precisely. They are pestiferous, self-glorious vipers.

SHAKESPEARE

Is that why you developed the Actor Ruse? You don't want to know how an actor might feel about a character you've created?

OXFORD

I just want you to speak the speech I pray you as I pronounced it to you. For anything so o'er done is from the purpose of playing, who's end, both at the first and now, was and is, to hold as 'twere, the mirror up to nature. And, Shakespeare, I abhor the groundlings, who for the most part are capable of nothing but inexplicable dumb shows and noise. Agreed?

SHAKESPEARE

Agreed. Touchy, touchy, touchy. I need another drink and better company.

Shakespeare gets up from the table and goes to another part of the tavern. Francis Bacon enters wearing a mask. He carries a leather satchel. He sits at Oxford's table.

OXFORD

I see where you got Kit Marlowe to go along with the Rosicrucian's death plan.

Bacon takes off his mask.

BACON

Not in the least. He fought us...he went kicking and screaming into that good night.

OXFORD

He didn't agree to die in the tavern brawl?

BACON

Hell no! I was able to get Ingram Frizer, Nicholas Skeres, and Robert Poley to bring him to Eleanor Bull's house in Depthford, but that is where his cooperation ended.

OXFORD

Aren't they also in the employ of the Queen's secret service?

BACON

Correct. I thought he might better acquiesce if he were among his friends and see the necessity for this plan.

OXFORD

I take it he would not lie down and die.

BACON

When they told him why they were there, he exploded. Screaming he was at the start of his career.

OXFORD

I heard he was arguing over the bill with Ingram.

BACON

Please. That is the story we concocted. Lucky for us, Ingram kept his equilibrium and was able to ward off Marlowe's erratic behavior.

OXFORD

So was Kit stabbed?

BACON

Over his right eye. It was the only way Ingram could stop him… the wound was not life threating. The coroner is on the Queen's payroll, William Danby, his report looks official.

OXFORD

So where did you ship him off to?

BACON

Italy. He wanted to go to Venice. We used the ship *Expedition*, disguised him as a Flemish immigrant, gave him gold and some books. Let the Italians have him. His emotions will fit in nicely with their culture.

OXFORD

Do you think he will stay quiet?

BACON

He has no choice. We are arranging for him to continue with his playwriting, using a different name. I thought we would add his plays to Shakespeare's list. The Queen is putting Marlowe on salary too. It is a generous sum, and I do not think he will want to ruin his capital income just to expose himself and have assassins looking for him in Venice. Too many Catholics.

OXFORD

What will happen to Ingram Frizer? He's charged with murder?

BACON

Yes, but we have arranged for the Queen to pardon all three, Ingram, Robert, and Nicholas. Ingram will be imprisoned for a month, then released.

OXFORD

Remind me not to play chess with you.

Bacon pulls a script out of his leather satchel.

BACON

Oxford, I have a script sent to me from Marlowe. But I think it has problems and needs a rewrite.

OXFORD

What's it called?

BACON

The Merchant of Paris. A comedy. He's got a Jewish character in it.

OXFORD

What is his fascination with Jews? *The Jew of Malta.* I asked him about it, but he was evasive.

BACON

You don't know his heritage, do you?

OXFORD

Tell me.

BACON

His father is Jewish.

OXFORD

The shoemaker is a Jew?

BACON

No. His real father, Roger Manwood.

OXFORD

Manwood, the judge? Manwood is a Jew?

BACON

A Marrano. A Jew living in secret here in England. There are a quite a few of them.

OXFORD

Bacon, I know about the Marranos.

BACON

Did you know that Roderigo Lopez is a Marrano?

OXFORD

The Queen's physician?

BACON

There are a number of Marranos in the royal court. The Queen likes their council, and they live here under her protection. Manwood had an affair with Marlowe's mother. How do you think he was able to pay for a college education? The Jew, his father, paid for it. The Queen knows everything.

OXFORD

You amaze me. How do you know all of this?

BACON

There are certain advantages to being a part of the Queen's inner circle.

OXFORD

I knew it, a shoemaker couldn't afford his son a college education.

BACON

Manwood has been guiding Kit Marlowe's career path from the beginning with the blessing of the Queen.

OXFORD

So Marlowe is a Jew.

BACON

Technically no. In the Jewish culture, your mother has to be a Jew.

OXFORD

But what Englishman believes that? If his father is a Jew, then Marlowe is a Jew.

BACON

In his new play, he has a prominent character who is a Jew and he asks for a pound of flesh from a non-Jew. A Goy. A Christian. As a consequence to a business deal. If the borrower cannot pay, he must give up a pound of his flesh. Marlowe really hates the French.

OXFORD

He's not an enthusiast for French cuisine either. He complains that they put sauce on everything.

BACON

Oxford, he has a scene where the Jew cuts off the merchant's hand.

OXFORD

He might as well be writing Titus Andronicus. How's the structure?

BACON

Structure is sound. But I think you and I should do a rewrite. We can't have a Christian lose his hand to a Jew.

OXFORD

Let's make it Venice instead of Paris. As a kind of nod to where Marlowe ended up.

BACON

Merchant of Venice. I like that. A salute to all the Rosicrusians, too.

OXFORD

What do you want me to rewrite?

BACON

He has a bit about gold, silver, and lead. Three suitors come to the girl in the story, Portia, and vie for her hand. Her father has presented them with a riddle. They must solve the riddle to win her hand. As written now, gold is the answer, and that seems too obvious to me. Let's use lead.

OXFORD

Who are her suitors?

BACON

The last is, of course, the hero. The first is a prince of Arragon. The second is a prince of Dusseldorf.

OXFORD

I hate Germany. Let's make one of the princes from Morocco. I like toying with the idea that maybe the audience will think she is going to have to marry a black man.

BACON

Good idea. I want you to work on the gold, silver, lead theme. The three suitors have three choices as to which precious metal represents the love of his future bride. Marlowe wrote gold…but we can be a little wittier than that. I'd like you to use your intellect. Can you figure out a way to make it lead? And make it poetic. Let the suitor figure out how lead represents true love. Make it flowery.

Bacon hands Oxford a few pages from the manuscript.

OXFORD

Nice challenge, Bacon.

BACON

There is a section I need a little help with too.

Bacon pulls some blank pages from his satchel, a bottle of ink, and a feathered pen.

OXFORD

Yes?

BACON

There is a courtroom scene. The lawyer defends the merchant. I'm thinking of having the character of Portia masquerade as a man. She will be that lawyer. She/he defends the merchant in the courtroom and uses the law to save his pound of flesh. If the woman defends the man, it will create a nice tension that she might not be smart enough to win.

OXFORD

You need help with what? How the law can work in his favor?

BACON

No, I've solved that problem. I have a nice plot twist too. In an earlier love scene, she gives her lover, Bassanio, a ring, and he swears he'll never to take it off.

OXFORD

But he gives the ring to the lawyer, which is really her.

BACON

Too obvious?

OXFORD

No, not at all. You told me there's a twist. Nice dramatic moment. Maybe we can add some humor, too.

BACON

It's given as payment.

OXFORD

Before the trial?

BACON

No, after the trial. So the Jew does not get his pound of flesh. The hero is obligated to give something of value to the lawyer.

OXFORD

I've got a good joke. Make the Jew convert to Christianity or he dies.

BACON

Big laugh. Good. I'll add it. Also, I want to send a message to the Queen.

OXFORD

What kind of message?

BACON

A message of mercy. Right now, in the royal court, she is in an awkward position. Lord Burghley is pressuring her to be strong and cruel. I think she should be merciful.

OXFORD

The Spanish incident?

BACON

Yes.

OXFORD

Let's write a speech about the qualities of mercy.

BACON

Or the quality of mercy...

OXFORD

Is not strained.

Bacon writes this down.

BACON

It drops like rain...

OXFORD

It droppeth as the gentle rain...Blank verse, my friend.

BACON

Yes, of course. "From Heaven." It droppeth as a gentle rain from heaven.

Bacon scratches out a line and writes a new line.

OXFORD

Yes. Good…very good. Let's use heaven as a metaphor. It droppeth as the gentle rain from heaven…

BACON

On the place below.

OXFORD

Upon the place beneath. It is twice blest. It blesses him that gives…

BACON

And him that takes.

OXFORD

Tis mightiest in the mightiest.

BACON

It becomes the throned monarch better than her crown.

OXFORD

Better than HIS crown. We don't want to be too obvious.

Bacon continues to write.

BACON

Wherein doth sit the dread and fear of Kings, but mercy is above this sceptered sway.

OXFORD

Wait, wait, listen to this: "It is enthroned in the hearts of Kings, It is the attribute to God Himself and earthly power doth then show likest God's when mercy seasons Justice."

BACON

Excellent, Oxford, excellent. If we do this right, the Queen cannot help but be moved.

OXFORD

The Merchant of Venice. I know some things about the city that I can add to the script…it will give it a more Italian flavor. I used to ask every morning, "What was the news on the Rialto?"

BACON

Yes. Nice touch. Here are the rest of the pages for the gold, silver, and lead scene.

Bacon hands some pages to Oxford. Oxford looks at the pages and figures out what he wants to say.

OXFORD

Thanks, we'll put Shakespeare's name on this…but let's not show it to him until we are ready to go into production.

BACON

I'll write Marlowe and let him know what we are doing.

Shakespeare comes over to the table with a pitcher of beer and three mugs.

SHAKESPEARE

Did I hear my new name? So how are my benefactors doing today?

BACON
The real question is how is our newly named and recent investment Shakespeare doing?

SHAKESPEARE
Spending your money on you. These drinks are on me.

Shakespeare pours drinks for everyone.

OXFORD
A toast to our new play, *Comedy of Errors.*

They all toast as Shakespeare joins them at the table.

SHAKESPEARE
Bacon, Oxford says he is going to put me in his next play. A role written especially for me.

BACON
I'm also writing a new play…and I'm sure I can develop a role for you.

SHAKESPEARE
I am in heaven. So I can be in it and you'll let me put my name on it as playwright too?

BACON
Shakespeare that is the contract we've made.

SHAKESPEARE
And you won't be upset with me getting all the accolades, both as actor and playwright?

BACON
Shakespeare, do you know Lady Elizabeth Hatton?

SHAKESPEARE

Not a clue.

BACON

Well, you don't really run in those social circles, do you?

OXFORD

Thank God.

BACON

When I say lady…it is actually an understatement. She comes from nobility. She is a virtuous lady. Her father, Thomas Cecil, was the first Earl of Exeter. She is married to the ailing William Hatton. Soon to be the widow Elizabeth Hatton. She has breeding, sophistication, and a lineage that connects her to the cream of British society. If any inkling of my theatre connection should waft its way back to her, my romantic plans are dashed.

SHAKESPEARE

But everybody loves the theatre.

BACON

No, my friend, not everyone. Of course, you love the theatre, but some English aristocrats find theatre distasteful. Elizabeth's delicate nose is offended by the stench that drifts up from the groundlings.

SHAKESPEARE

So you're saying she doesn't like a good laugh or enjoy a story well told?

BACON

Young Thespus…some English citizens of a noble class do not want to mix or mingle with the common man.

SHAKESPEARE

Snobs.

BACON

I once had dinner at Grey's Inn with the fine-featured, porcelain-faced Lady Elizabeth and we talked about Art.

OXFORD

Sounds like she took your breath away.

BACON

Every time I see her.

SHAKESPEARE

ART? You mean painters like DaVinci?

BACON

Yes, famous paintings, Well, crafted sonnets, Thomas Tallis's music, and alas, rowdy and rambunctious theatre.

SHAKESPEARE

I don't think theatre is so rambunctious.

OXFORD

You wouldn't.

BACON

As we sat dining on our mutton and drinking red wine, she expressed her disdain for the low characters that show up at a theatre. You know, reprobates, cut purses, harlots, and pimps.

SHAKESPEARE

Gypsies, tramps, and thieves.

BACON

Exactly. I wanted to invite her to a play I had written…but it became obviously clear, very quickly that if she knew I was connected to the theatre in any substantial way, my romantic options would evaporate, as mist in the morning dew.

SHAKESPEARE

Oh, hodge-pudding!

BACON

My having a Parliament seat in Middlesex is a blessing and an asset.

SHAKESPEARE

In her eyes.

BACON

As is my ambition to strive for Her Majesty's Attorney General. But any whiff of me supporting English Theatre might dash my hopes of an Aristocratic marriage.

OXFORD

Beware of Edward Coke. He is devious.

BACON

It is no secret that I am not the only gentleman who has husbandly eyes set on her as a goal. My competition for Lady Elizabeth's hand is Edward Coke…but he is a mean-spirited, royal-court Rampallian. He just wants her money and her titles.

OXFORD

No doubt.

BACON

I actually love her.

SHAKESPEARE

Sir Francis, then I suppose you're not coming to the opening of *Comedy of Errors*.

BACON

Yes. I will be there.

SHAKESPEARE

I assume without Lady Elizabeth Hatton.

BACON

You assume correctly.

SHAKESPEARE

Eddy, you want to show Sir Francis our actor ruse?

BACON

What kind of ruse?

SHAKESPEARE

The Actor Ruse. Because I'm the playwright, I get the questions about the play. Sometimes, the actors want to change a line or they may have a plot question. Eddy here is paying for everything, so we double team them. I don't know what Eddy wants me to say to them, so I consider the question, then walk around the theatre mumbling, then I defer to Eddy 'cause he's the money, and he gives the answer. We'll show you. Ask us an actor question.

BACON

I don't think my character would say this line.

Shakespeare jumps up from the table and starts pacing and mumbling what Bacon has just said.

SHAKESPEARE

He doesn't think his character would say that line. HE doesn't think his character would say that line. He doesn't THINK his character would say that line. He doesn't think his CHARACTER would say that line. He doesn't think his character WOULD SAY that line.

Suddenly, he stops and bends over and whispers into Oxford's ear. Oxford listens.

OXFORD
Yes. He would.

SHAKESPEARE
See. We're a team, Eddy and me.

BACON
I see. The real playwright makes the decision without the actors realizing what you two have done. Uh, Shakespeare, do me a favor. Show a little more respect to the seventeenth Earl of Oxford. Call him Sir Edward or Lord DeVere or your Lordship. But not Eddy.

SHAKESPEARE
I did not mean to offend his lordship; I just feel so close to him. Like the big brother I never had.

OXFORD
Let's toast to the opening of *Comedy of Errors*.

They all raise their mugs.

OXFORD, BACON, SHAKESPEARE
To *Comedy of Errors*.

Black Out.

Scene 3

Shakespeare enters the Mermaid Tavern. He is elated. It is December 28, 1594. There has just been an afternoon performance of Comedy of Errors at Greys Inn Hall.

SHAKESPEARE
What a day? What a day! First thanks for the stipend. What a performance! Oxford, it was the best opening ever.

Oxford enters.

OXFORD
Enjoyed yourself, didn't you?

SHAKESPEARE
Ben Johnson, the playwright, came to me and complimented me on my sense of humor.
He said he loved all the funny lines. Ben Johnson! He's my new best friend.

OXFORD
Good feeling.

SHAKESPEARE
He kept quoting the line, "Satan come forth." Then he'd laugh and say, "Great line."

OXFORD

Heady feeling.

SHAKESPEARE

I must admit I had my doubts about the fourth act, but it all came together beautifully. Oxford…you are a very funny guy. Dromio simply priceless.

OXFORD

Which one?

SHAKESPEARE

Both! *Comedy of Errors*. Promise me you'll publish it with my name.

OXFORD

Guaranteed.

SHAKESPEARE

Love it! Love it. Love it. An actor came up to me and introduced himself, looking for a job. Wants me to consider him for my next play. Isn't that hysterical?

OXFORD

Who?

SHAKESPEARE

Some fellow named Richard Burbage. He kept insisting he was a wonderful actor.

OXFORD

What did you say?

SHAKESPEARE

I told him that I thought he might be a robustious peri-wig pated fellow. I asked would he tear a passion to tatters, to very rags?

OXFORD

His answer?

SHAKESPEARE

Only if I want him too. I like that…robustious peri-wig pated fellow.
We should put that in a future play.

OXFORD

By the way, how is your son Hamnet doing?

SHAKESPEARE

Much better. I think he is going to be all right. The money helped.

Bacon enters the tavern. He sits with Shakespeare and Oxford.

BACON

Ah, Shakespeare, glad you're here. Oxford, I want you to listen to this and tell me what you think.

SHAKESPEARE

What is it?

BACON

A speech from my new play. It's a comedy.

SHAKESPEARE

What's the premise?

BACON

Just listen and I will fill you in after you hear what I've written. This is a lord talking to a lady.

SHAKESPEARE

What did he do to her?

BACON

He lied…so did HIS friends…lie to HER friends.

SHAKESPEARE

So he's trying to beg forgiveness? For everybody?

BACON

Shakespeare, just listen:
"Honest plain words best pierce the ear of grief
And by these badges understand the KING
For your fair sakes have we neglected time
Played foul play with our oaths. Your beauty ladies,
Hath much DEFORMED us, fashioning our humor
Even to the opposed end of our intents;
And what in us had seemed ridiculous
As love is full of unbefitting strains
All wanton as a child, skipping and vain."

SHAKESPEARE

Clever rhyme. Stains and vain.

BACON

Let me finish:
"Formed by the eye and therefore like the eye,
Full of strange shapes, of habits and of forms
Varying in subjects as the eye doth roll
To every varied object in his glance;
Which parti-coated presence of loose love
Put on by us, if, in your heavenly eyes
Have mis-becomed our oaths and gravities,
Those heavenly eyes that look into these faults
Suggested us to make."

SHAKESPEARE

Brilliant use of "eyes," Bacon. Brilliant. The "eyes" have it.

BACON

Not done, Shakespeare. Keep listening.
"Therefore, ladies,
Our love being yours the error that love makes
is likewise yours. We to ourselves prove false
by being once false, forever to be true
to those that make us both...fair ladies, you
and even that a falsehood, in itself a sin
thus, purifies itself and turns to grace."

OXFORD

Beautiful. I like it. Bacon.

SHAKESPEARE

I think it sounds beautiful...but you should have a couplet that rhymes with sin at the end. Something like: and even that a falsehood, in itself a sin,
One kiss from you is all I need to win.

BACON

The speech is in the middle of the scene. We save the couplets for the end of the scene.

SHAKESPEARE

Oh, right. I keep forgetting. I've got an idea for a play. If I write it, will you, gentlemen, take a look at it. I think I could do as well as you.

BACON

NO...NO...NO.

OXFORD

I wouldn't rush down that road, if I were you. Wisely and slow, they stumble that run fast. Just enjoy the lifestyle we are helping to provide you.

SHAKESPEARE

I do. Honestly, gentlemen, I do…but I have a few ideas I might scribble down and just let you take a look at. I can take criticism. Honestly, I can. I've got this idea for three witches and a soldier. So these three witches tell this soldier that they think he will be king.

BACON

NO. NO. NO. A pox on your throat, you bawling, blasphemous, in charitable dog!

SHAKESPEARE

Wait, Bacon, just hear me out. His wife is a real shrew. A bitch. So she insists that he kill the King who has stopped over to their castle for a good night's rest. But this canker-sore wants to be Queen so baldly, her ambition pushes him into murdering their King. Good idea, right?

BACON

Here's a criticism, Shakespeare…NO! I DON'T LIKE IT!

SHAKESPEARE

Trust me when it comes to writing a shrew, I know I can do this. I have first-hand experience. She could say something like "Come, you spirits that tend on mortal thoughts UNSEX me here, and fill me from the crown to the toe, top-full of direst cruelty!" Now, tell me…is that a shrew line or not?

OXFORD

That's a mean woman.

SHAKESPEARE

Damn right, she's mean! Believe me, I know how to write that woman firsthand. Plus, I have a woman that lives three doors down from me. She says she is a real witch. She can give me some authentic incantations and we can put them in the play.

BACON

Authentic incantations? Bad Luck!

SHAKESPEARE

She has told me stories that have left me bewitched, bothered, and bewildered.

BACON

I don't like it. Shakespeare, you're just a front. A façade. The beard…we pay you to let us use your name. Let's not change the contract in the middle of the game.

SHAKESPEARE

Bacon, all that talk in your writing. I just don't get it. I think some of your work needs more action. A sword fight or maybe somebody getting poisoned.

BACON

Are you forgetting my latest play is a comedy?

SHAKESPEARE

Oh yes, right…but my play has action. Murder, sword fights. The groundlings like action.

OXFORD

Maybe you have to see, Bacon's comedy mounted.

SHAKESPEARE

Maybe.

BACON

Don't worry. It will all become clear soon. This is the play we are going to do next.

SHAKESPEARE

So my name will go on this?

BACON

Yes, of course.

SHAKESPEARE

So what kind of comedy is this?

BACON

It's a love story.

SHAKESPEARE

No sword fighting?

BACON

Kills the joke.

SHAKESPEARE

No poison either, I guess?

BACON

Three noble kinsmen promise their king they will be celibate.

SHAKESPEARE

How can it be a love story if the men promise to be celibate?

BACON

They promise the king they'll be celibate for three years…then a princess and three lovely ladies show up in the kingdom. The men labor for their love.

SHAKESPEARE

They labor for love? They're celibate? That sounds like love's labor lost! I hope this is a really funny comedy.

BACON

A comedy with wit, word play, and wasted love. Have you heard of the poet Sir Phillip Sidney?

OXFORD

He was my ex-enemy, Shakespeare, and the author of *The Countess of Penbroke's Arcania*.

BACON

The Queen loves his writing…and I have written this play as a nod to his genius. Sydney's ability to use words in a creative way. The first performance of this play will be this Christmas in the Queen's Royal Court.

OXFORD

Would you like to meet the Queen, Shakespeare?

SHAKESPEARE

If my wife could only hear what you just asked. Yes, a thousand times yes.

BACON

We will introduce you to her as the author of this play.

SHAKESPEARE

Me, standing in the Royal Court. Rubbing elbows with the royal elite.

OXFORD

You won't be as impressed when you actually meet them. Bacon, I saw Lord Burghley today after the performance. We talked about the play, he loved the writing and the jokes. He had no idea that I wrote it. Those are my jokes. He wanted to meet Shakespeare here. Thinks you're a genius. It took all my composure to hold my laughter in.

BACON
Feels good, doesn't it. Say what you want and no one is the wiser.

OXFORD
I am definitely publishing *Venus and Adonis* with your name on it.

SHAKESPEARE
Thank you, Oxford. Do you have a new play that you are working on?

OXFORD
I am writing a play that will have fairies interacting with humans. I want to play with the idea of the fairies' world colliding with the reality of our world.

SHAKESPEARE
Wait, wait, wait, you want fairies interacting with humans?

OXFORD
It takes place in Athens, in the summer. Maybe have a common workman, a peasant, being seduced by a Fairy Queen.

SHAKESPEARE
Hold it, hold it, hold it…A Queen makes love to a common man?

OXFORD
Yes. A mechanical. Specifically, a Weaver.

SHAKESPEARE
How is that going to work? Fairies and humans talking to each other?

OXFORD
Yes, in Athens. A Greek comedy.

SHAKESPEARE
That's good.

OXFORD

And since most men are asses. The common man will have the head of an ass, when the queen makes love to him.

SHAKESPEARE

Fools and fairies. You think all men asses? Maybe, she's hitting rock bottom.

OXFORD

His name will be Rock Bottom.

SHAKESPEARE

Just call him Rock.

BACON

Just call him Bottom.

SHAKESPEARE

So Bottom, who has the face of an Ass, makes love to a Fairie Queen…how does that happen?

OXFORD

I don't know. That's what I am working on.

SHAKESPEARE

Make it a dream. I've had dreams like that.

BACON

Wet dreams?

SHAKESPEARE

Yes, of course. So a Bottom gets made love to by…a Fairie…in Greece, in the summer time?

OXFORD

Essentially…I also want to do a play within the play. "The lamentable comedy and most cruel death of Pyramus and Thisby."

SHAKESPEARE

What is this soon to be masterpiece called?

OXFORD

I don't have a title for it yet.

SHAKESPEARE

How about *A Midnight Dream in Summer*?

OXFORD

Maybe.

SHAKESPEARE

At this rate, we will have a play every year for the next twenty years. Mercy, mercy me, things aren't what they used to be.

Shakespeare takes a folded piece of paper out of his pocket.

SHAKESPEARE

Do you know what that is?

Oxford and Bacon stare at the paper.

OXFORD

A sonnet?

SHAKESPEARE

No. It's a love letter…from my wife! She thanks me for the money, and she heard I wrote a play that was being performed in London. I am becoming famous and her whole outlook and perception of me has changed.

OXFORD

Congratulations. Good news!

SHAKESPEARE

She used to have disdain and contempt for me.

BACON

And now she doesn't. The residue of being famous. Shakespeare, enjoy it.

SHAKESPEARE

But it's false. I can remember countless times she looked down her nose at me and clucked her tongue when I expressed a thought that gave me pleasure.

OXFORD

Shakespeare, now you have a wife that honors you, enjoy it.

SHAKESPEARE

Honors me? More honored in the breach than the observance. Oxford, you ever tell a friend a favorite story and have your wife say, "Not that old story again?" Then as you tell the story, she moans and groans through the telling?

OXFORD

Yes, I know she has a minor contempt for you and your stories... but those days are gone now.

BACON

Yes. With your newfound fame, she will now listen intently and applaud your story-telling skills...because you are famous.

Shakespeare takes out another piece of paper from a different pocket.

SHAKESPEARE

Bacon...do you know what that is?

BACON

A sonnet?

SHAKESPEARE

No! It's a love letter.

OXFORD

Your wife certainly is in a loving mood.

SHAKESPEARE

This comes from a new friend. A Dark Lady. She came to a rehearsal, loved what she saw, and wrote me this letter.

BACON

You have an admirer. Does this Dark Lady have a name?

SHAKESPEARE

Lucy Negro!

OXFORD

Black Luce, the brothel owner in Clerkenwell?

SHAKESPEARE

She loves the theatre. She loves my writing. She wants me to write her sonnets.

OXFORD

Now that is a real Comedy of Errors.

SHAKESPEARE

This fame crown is not as easy to wear as I thought it might be.

OXFORD

Uneasy sits the head that wears the crown.

BACON

We have one more playwright we'd like you to front for.

SHAKESPEARE

Do I know him?

BACON / OXFORD

No!No!

BACON

He's our friend…but he's out of the country.

OXFORD

He's an Englishman and wants to get his plays done here…even though he is away.

SHAKESPEARE

That's odd. What's his name?

BACON

Shakespeare, part of this arrangement is that where we can keep the secrets; we must keep them. I cannot tell you his name. You must trust that we like his playwrighting and he has important things to say.

OXFORD

We promised we'd help him get his plays produced.

BACON

He went to Italy and fell in love with the country. The cuisine, the people…

SHAKESPEARE

The religion. He's Catholic, isn't he? He can't practice his religion here because of the Queen, right?

OXFORD

Can't get anything past you, Shakespeare.

SHAKESPEARE

I understand politics.

BACON

We told him about you. If he can have an alias, he can write freely and not worry about censorship.

SHAKESPEARE

I'll agree as long as he doesn't say anything against Protestants and the Queen. I don't want my head on a platter.

OXFORD

We'll let you read every word before it is spoken on stage.

BACON

Plus, we are going to increase your payment. It will be worth it. Your name will become the banner for good theatre.

OXFORD

Trust us, Shakespeare, this Englishman is a good writer.

SHAKESPEARE

I feel like I should know this man. An English playwright. Are you sure I don't know him?

BACON / OXFORD

Positive.Absolutely.

A beat they look at each other. Then…

BACON /OXFORD

Absolutely.Positive.

SHAKESPEARE

Does he have a new play he wants done here?

BACON

Yes. He sent me a first draft of a new manuscript.

OXFORD

Oh. He did?

BACON

Yes.

OXFORD

What's the premise?

BACON

Since being in Italy, he's really gotten into the customs and the culture of the country. He's discovered an old Italian legend which he wants to turn into a play.

OXFORD

Which old Italian legend?

BACON

He's written a play about *Romeo and Juliet.*

OXFORD

That's been done and redone and overdone. Surely, he can't be serious.

BACON

Trust me, he is serious…and I don't think he can be talked out of it.

OXFORD

Well, Shakespeare, I don't think you have to worry about offending Protestants and the Queen.

SHAKESPEARE

Good.

OXFORD

Just boring a few theatre patrons, with a tired overworn tale.

BACON

Actually, he's got quite a nice view on it. And he's given Romeo a best friend, Mercutio. Quite flamboyant. I think the character is a scene stealer.

OXFORD

I have to read it…before I believe that.

BACON

We ALL will. But the blank verse is exceptional. He asked me if I would contact Edward Allyn to play Mercutio.

SHAKESPEARE

Allyn, isn't he Marlowe's man?

BACON

Since Marlowe's dead…I'm sure he won't mind being employed by us.

SHAKESPEARE

Is there a role in the play for me?

BACON

Actually, there is. Romeo's confidant, Friar Lawrence.

SHAKESPEARE

Then I am good.

OXFORD

This calls for a celebration! We have a triumph with *Comedy of Errors.*

BACON

We have the promise of a production for the Queen, this Christmas with my new play, *Love Labour's...*

SHAKESPEARE

Lost! And I've got a growing reputation in the theatre and money in my purse.

OXFORD

I think this new partnership, which is working so well, deserves a toast.
Gentlemen, raise your glasses! A toast to English Theatre.

They all raise their glasses.

BACON

And a couplet for the end.

OXFORD

If our writing has offended.
Think but this and all is mended.

BACON
That you have but endured here.
While we visions did appear.

OXFORD
And this weak and idle theme.

SHAKESPEARE
Is not exactly what it seems.

BACON
Gentles, do not reprehend.

OXFORD
If you pardon, we will mend.

BACON
And as I am an honest scribe.
Take our words, not as a bribe.

SHAKESPEARE
Else this scribe a liar call.
So good night unto you all.

They clink their glasses.

BACON / OXFORD / SHAKESPEARE
To English Theatre!

Black Out.

END OF PLAY

The Cause, My Soul

The Prequel to Othello
Written in Iambic Pentameter

Dedicated to

My Lovely Wife,
Mary Lange

The Cause, My Soul opened April 23, 2016, at the Odyssey Theatre, Los Angele, California, with the following cast:

DESDEMONA	Lindsey Santefort
RODERIGO	Steve Ducey
EMILIA	Jessica Moreno
IAGO	Stephen Spiegel
THE DUKE OF VENICE	Bruce Cervi
BRABANTIO	Gordon Goodman
CASSIO	Michael Proctor, William Reinbold
OTHELLO	Thomas Anthony Jones
BIANCA	Keena Ferguson, Chrystee Pharris
THE PRIEST	Paul Messinger
LADY MARY	Mary Lange

Director	Ted Lange
Set Designer	Pete Hickok
Costume Designer	Mylette Nora
Wardrobe Master	Wendell Carmichael
Lighting Designer	Alex Freer
Sound Designer	Will Mahood
Lighting and Sound Tech	Steve Norris
Stage Manager	Mary Lange

The Cause, My Soul opened August 1, 2017, at the Hainesbrand Theatre in Winston-Salem, North Carolina, at the National Black Theatre Festival with the following cast:

DESDEMONA	Cynthia Aldrich
RODERIGO	Steve Ducey
EMILIA	Jessica Moreno
IAGO	Stephen Spiegel
THE DUKE OF VENICE	Bruce Cervi
BRABANTIO	Gordon Goodman
CASSIO	Michael Proctor
OTHELLO	Thomas Anthony Jones
BIANCA	Chrystee Pharris
THE PRIEST	Paul Messinger
LADY MARY	Mary Lange

Director	Ted Lange
Set Designer	Pete Hickok
Costume Designer	Mylette Nora
Wardrobe Master	Wendell Carmichael
Sound Designer	Will Mahood
Stage Manager	Mary Lange

AUTHOR'S NOTE

In 2015, I traveled to Edinburg, Scotland, from Los Angeles, via Winston-Salem, North Carolina, where I had just finished mounting one of my plays for the National Black Theatre Festival. I was jet-lagged and pressed to make sure the play I was directing, *Waitless* by Cailin Harrison starring Jessica Moreno and Andrew Boyle, could be set up, staged, and broken down within the seventy-minute time allotted for each production in the Edinburg Fringe Festival. The venue for *Waitless* was a church where ten other plays were also being mounted. After a couple of time-challenged days, our play opened and I finally began to process the diversity and creativity of the other shows in our venue. One that instantly grabbed my interest was a prequel to *Macbeth* called *Incarnate*. It included four witches instead of three, and the prequel concept instantly captivated my writer's mind-set. I had already written twenty-two plays and when I bragged to my wife, Mary, that I could write a prequel to a Shakespearean play, she, of course, called me to the carpet and questioned, "And what Shakespearean prequel would you write?" Without a second's hesitation, I responded, "*Othello*," and as soon as I said that, the entire play flashed through my consciousness. I started writing that night...

My history with the play, *Othello*, began in 1984 as an acting student at London's Royal Academy of Dramatic Arts, where I was asked to study the role of Othello. A year before I was directing an episode of *Love Boat* and Lynn Redgrave was a guest star. While we were waiting for a scene to be lit, we started exchanging some Shakespearean lines. I had been cast as Romeo post high school and had just finished directing *Hamlet* in Los Angeles. She taunted me that "serious" Shakespearean actors all study at RADA, the Royal Academy of Dramatic Arts in London. A year later, I was in London doing just that because I certainly considered myself a serious Shakespearean actor.

At RADA, we were asked to pick a scene to perform for the class. I wanted to do a scene from *Richard the III* as Richard or from *Henry the IV* as Falstaff, roles not commonly offered to black actors, but Othello prevailed. After studying the play, multiple questions surfaced: the motivation for Othello's actions, the depth of his love for Desdemona, and the impetus for Iago's villainy. I continued my journey with *Othello* in 1989, where I performed as Othello at the Inner-City Cultural Center in Los Angeles and later that year, I directed and starred, as the first American black actor, in an independent film version of *Othello*. After RADA, I realized that while the English viewed aspects of Shakespeare's plays as obvious conclusions, Americans regarded them as oblique.

Back to my present Othello foray, I challenged myself to write the prequel in verse and address the issues that had surfaced for me at RADA while educating American audiences in the English viewpoint. I retained the integrity of the characters crafted by Shakespeare and explored the flirtation, romance, comedy, and drama of Othello's journey into love and politics. I also explored the seeds of Iago's treachery and created plausible assumptions from what takes place in *Othello*.

To introduce the play, I open with the courtship of Desdemona and Roderigo. *When did Roderigo and Desdemona meet?* In Shakespeare's *Othello*, we never see them together we only hear about Roderigo's attempts at wooing Desdemona. The purpose of this scene is to show the incompatibility of Roderigo and Desdemona and see how Othello's persona will ultimately be a better match.

The life of Iago started with the premise that Iago is a nice guy who has just returned from fighting and is anxious to reunite with his wife. Instead of welcoming him into her bed, Emilia protests and sends him off to a tavern under the guise of properly preparing for a reunion.

Emilia, in truth, has her sights set on the Black Moor, and Iago, none the wiser for the moment, complies.

I referenced the text in *Othello* to build upon and create the actions taken by the same characters in the prequel. For example, part of Iago's motivation for his villainy is that he thinks Othello has slept with his wife, Emilia. He mentions this twice, Act I, scene 3, line 385: "I hate the Moor and it is thought abroad that 'twixt my sheets he's done my office."

The second quote is Act II, Scene 1, line 293.

> "But partly to diet my revenge
> For that I do suspect the lusty Moor,
> Hath leapt into my seat: the thought whereof
> Doth, like a poisonous mineral, gnaw at my inwards
> And nothing can or shall content my soul
> Till I am even'd with him wife for wife;
> Or failing so, yet that I put the Moor
> at least into a jealousy so strong
> That judgement cannot cure."

In the prequel, I corroborate the relationship between Emilia and Othello. I have taken a stand on vague moments that the English view as *choices.*

Now, it is time for Othello to enter majestically in his element. Othello, a mercenary, meets the Duke and Brabantio to get his reward for his work in the army accompanied by Michael Cassio, his arithmetician/soldier. The Duke has told Brabantio about some of Othello's stories. Brabantio invites Othello to dine at his home. Thus, a chance to meet the lovely Desdemona.

The courtship of Othello and Desdemona displays their instant chemistry, but poses the conundrum of Othello converting from Islam to Christianity. The English know that being a Moor, Othello's religion is Islam and that he must convert to Christianity for Desdemona. The joy of creating the next scene is the meeting of Othello and the Priest where he tells him of his plan to convert to Christianity and wed Desdemona.

The two men argue over the Holy Bible versus the Holy Quran regarding the story of Abraham. In the Holy Bible, it is Abraham's son, Isaac, that is going to be sacrificed. In the Holy Quran, it is Abraham's son, Ishme'al. Same story, two different points of view.

My prequel is set to interlace the tale in *The Cause, My Soul* and culminate at the start of Shakespeare's *Othello*.

SYNOPSIS

E very love story has a beginning…

"Dost thou have a tale that can be mine?" asks Desdemona.

The flirtation, the romance, the comedy, and the drama of Othello's journey into love and politics ensues in *The Prequel to Othello, The Cause, My Soul*. How does the flirtation begin? How does Othello woo Desdemona? Why does Othello promote Cassio instead of Iago? Were Othello and Emilia lovers? How did Roderigo and Iago meet? Why does Bianca want to marry Cassio? Was Othello a Muslim before he was a Christian? *The Cause, My Soul* explores the plausible interrelationships of these characters before the events in Shakespeare's play, *Othello*. Remaining true to the characters crafted by Shakespeare, this tale unfolds in 1571, yet is timeless and relevant to our current-day society.

Othello replies, "I could weave you a tale that would make thine heart shutter, make thine eyes dance in glory."

DRAMATIS PERSONAE

Desdemona is Brabantio's daughter (twenty years old).

Roderigo is Desdemona's suitor (twenty years old).

Emilia is Iago's wife (thirty years old).

Iago is an ancient (ensign) in Othello's army (thirty years old).

The Duke of Venice is a politician (fifty years old).

Brabantio is a senator of Venice and Desdemona's father (sixty years old).

Cassio is an honorable soldier in Othello's army (thirty years old).

Othello, The Moor is a general in the service of Venice (forty years old).

Bianca is a courtesan from Cyprus (thirty years old).

Priest is a Catholic Father (fifty years old).

Lady Mary is a lady-in-waiting.

THE CURTAIN SPEECH

If thou dost seek the inclination to
withdraw from this establishment, o please,
wilt thou journey through the portals marked in
our reptilian green with the letters
E.X.I.T.

Alas poor Samsung, I knew it
Horatio, a devise of infinite
possibilities that always chooses
to exalt itself in such moments of
inopportunity. We would hope you
groundlings will choose to abate its potential
by extinguishing the audible
proclivities it tends to make.

We of this company do invite you within this wooden 'O'
to revel in our antics and enjoy, *The Cause, My Soul.*

**Spoken on April 23, 2016, by the playwright at the Odyssey
Theatre, Los Angeles, California.**

Yes, t'was four-hundred years ago today
our William Shakespeare had his final say.

T'was born and died on April twenty-third,
a playwright the whole world had known and heard.

From this stage, we celebrate his noble past,
for we know his art is timeless and vast.

We of this company invite you
within this wooden 'O',
to revel in our antics and enjoy,
The Cause, My Soul.

ACT I

Scene 1

The year is 1571 in the city of Venice, Italy. Casa Di Brabantio: Roderigo is wooing Desdemona.

DESDEMONA
My father tells me I'm too young to wed.

RODERIGO
He will approve. I am perfect for your heart.

DESDEMONA
Ask me in a year. I can't now decide.

RODERIGO
I will pamper thee. I will shower thee
with gifts. My money will fill all of thy
earthly needs, and I will fill all of thy
desires, whims, thoughts of husbandly deeds.

DESDEMONA
Roderigo, tempt not with talk of gold.
Thou know'st I am not ruled by possessions.
O, woo not me with golden promises.
I want to see your romantic side, please.
Woo me with words of rhyme and metaphor.
Be a poet for me.

RODERIGO

I can do that.
I am a wonderful writer, 'tis true.
I am full of words. Long words, short words, too.
I will write thee sonnets. Sonnets of love.
Words of adventure. The adventures we
will face together, as husband and wife.
In school, prizes were given for writing.
I was known as a wonderful writer.

DESDEMONA

So then, let me hear one of your school poems.

RODERIGO

There was a sad maiden from Rome,
who wanted to call Venice her home.
She travelled far and wide,
but her parents could never decide.
So she married a Spaniard named Sid
and they all moved with him to Madrid
where they lived in a home with a copper dome.
And that's what I call a wonderful poem.

DESDEMONA

Roderigo, do not bore with limericks.
Let us not play in the past. Write me a
stanza for today. O, show me thy mind.
Teach me to love thy imagination.
Give me stories, write for me like Tasso
Be my Torquato Tasso, sing lyrics.
Look into thy heart and open the best
part of thyself…that I might see thy soul.

RODERIGO

I will write thee an epic poem of love.
Would not Homer cry if he could hear it?
He'd cry and wished he could have told this tale.
The Iliad will pale by comparison,
The Odyssey will appear lackluster,
next to my words, all others will fall down.

DESDEMONA

What if I crave a sonnet, Roderigo?

RODERIGO

I will write a fantastical sonnet.
I will shower thee with raindrops of words.
Words that will pour down from my mouth, for thee,
like a cloudburst. Yes, my Desdemona,
I am thine's. I speak with a poet's heart.
I am a man of great substance. A man
of wealth and proper Italian station.
All the women of Venice do love me.

DESDEMONA

They love thee or do they love thy money?

RODERIGO

O, what does it matter, why they love me?
I love thee. I promise thou will learn to
love all of my potential. We will have
a spectacular wedding. Yes, we will.
All Venice will sing hosannas to us.
O, we will wed at San Biagio.
I'll have Bishop Lugano marry us.
He made a promise, I was an altar boy.

DESDEMONA

Promises, promises…more promises.
Please leave me, ere I die of promises.

RODERIGO

I leave thee, sweet lady, when I return,
the depth of my promises, shall be seen.

Now I leave to write my loving words down.
Tell your seamstress, prepare the wedding gown.

Black Out.

Scene 2

Casa di Iago: Emilia is sitting in a chair, sipping wine. There is a broom at her feet.

EMILIA

Let me tell you of our state of affairs,
let me share with you all my wifely thoughts.
The Cyprus war has not ended, but now
our men return home from the battlefield.
My husband, I not have seen for two years.
He's Othello's ancient prized aide, strong arm.
I know after two years, his appetite
will be at its peak. I will be used.
Men. Husbands. Lovers. A bride's time needs her
groom. He'll desire me to dust his broom,
yet I want to guide the time of when and
how, my choice, not his.

IAGO

Emilia! *(off stage)*

EMILIA *(she quickly starts sweeping)*
Ah, see where he comes.

IAGO *(enters)*
Wife, show thyself. I am back from the wars.

EMILIA

My love, thou look'st no worse, than when thou left.

IAGO

Luck and skill followed me into battle.

They kiss.

EMILIA

As Othello's ancient, your duty was done.

IAGO

And now to bed. I have hungered for thee.

EMILIA

O, not yet, Iago. Let us wait 'till night.

IAGO

Emilia, I have been gone for years,
and now, thou refuse thy wifely duty?

EMILIA

'Tis not a refusal, a postponement.
I want to freshen up. Bathe, perfume, rest,
so that I might be at my best for thee.

IAGO

O, I am hungry. Will take thy worst.
I will take thou sleep or take thou awake.
This cursed demon must release my loins.

EMILIA

Oh, let it be later, strong Iago.
Thy Emilia could only think of thee,
how soon would her errant knight return.

Wanting thee to bury your pride in my joy.
And with each stroke, I will cry out thy name.
Iago, Iago, oh yes, my Iago, yes.
But I have been about the house today,
cleaning, working, sweating, and now the smell
of my day's chores haunts me even now.
O, please, let us wait 'till the sun has set.
We will light candles and linger in each
other's arms. 'Till we see the sun rise again.

IAGO

That does sound appetizing to me now.

EMILIA

Trust me, good husband. Give me a chance
to rest from today's work and to pamper
my body, perfume all my lady parts.
Yes, thy wait will be amply rewarded.
Take drink with thy comrades. Enjoy the time
'twill make the suspense of what is coming
instead of what cannot be right now.

IAGO

A drink? Yes, a drink, 'tis good to have drink.
Time with my comrades, then a return home.
A hot night filled with Kama Sutra poses.

EMILIA

Husband, we will start with the *Tiger's Tooth*,
and travel the path of *Flower in Bloom*.
Go to thy friends. And when the sun has set,
your walk in my garden will quench thy thirst.

IAGO

I am a better man for not taking
thee now, and a smarter man for knowing
thy promises are not idle claims, love.
For yes, I remember our wedding night.

EMILIA

That was a night filled with laughter, romance,
and too much wine. As I'm honest, I prepare.
Now go, Ancient, go. Come back to thy wife
at sunset. Tonight, we will play 'till stars,
laugh at our loving antics. They will smile.
Play with thy friends, so that later, on your
return I will play with your friend, gladly.

She kisses him and grabs his crotch.

IAGO

Ancient now, but I return lieutenant.

EMILIA

Why? How is this true?

IAGO

The Moor is in need.
We lost an officer, now the Black Moor
must choose a new lieutenant to captain
his troops. No doubt, I am the perfect choice.

EMILIA

Good news, my husband. Lieutenant's salary!
M'lord, tis by far a much better reward.
Tis a reward that my IAGO has earned.

IAGO

True, I have done many deeds for the Moor.
He knows it. I can think of no one whose
fingers fit that glove better than my own.
But I will have insurance. I know of
three mediators who the Moor does trust.
T'will have them intercede on my behalf.
He can't but say yes with such high acclaim.

EMILIA

Thou hast always been loyal, true, forthright,
and honest. Thou delight me my husband.
This news maketh tonight's excursion all
the more satisfying. So go…now go,
have drink, relax thy thoughts, and then tonight
thy wife will wash away all frustrations.
I will see thee in a prime state of mind,
look and seek, my honey is what you'll find.

Black Out.

Scene 3

Palazzo Ducale: Enter the Duke. Enter Brabantio, with a chest filled with sacks of gold.

DUKE

Do we have his reward?

BRABANTIO

Yes, my Lordship.

Brabantio taps the chest with his hand.

BRABANTIO

This chest contains his golden commission.

DUKE

We must keep our black friend a happy man.

BRABANTIO

We are not overpaying him, are we?

DUKE

He fights battles no Venetian general
will fight. True, he is a very wise man.
A talented tactician, and he wins.
He accepts his gold at the end of day
not at the start of the morning, my friend.
If he doesn't return, we have lost nothing.

BRABANTIO

But he always returns, M'lord. Always.

DUKE

How he wins, sometimes is a wonderment
to me? Have you heard him tell his dark tales?

BRABANTIO

No, M'lord. I have not had the pleasure.

DUKE

Well, Brabantio, he weaves wonderful
stories of adventure. Sometime you must
have him to dinner. He is masterful.
He has an arsenal of adventures.

BRABANTIO

Yes, M'lord.

DUKE

I thank our stars we found this Blackamoor.
He has secured the safety of Venice
and given the citizens a hero.

BRABANTIO

For a black, he is very talented.

DUKE

I care not about his color as long
as he wins. We pay him for his success.
He secures the values of our state
A true hero. Our Venetian generals,
They would do well to mark his example.
Ah, good, Brabantio, see where he comes.

Othello wearing a taqiyah enters with Cassio.

OTHELLO

Most potent, brave, and generous signors,
my very noble and approved good masters.
I have return'd triumphant to your city.

DUKE

No, my brave Othello, our city.
As agreed, here is your payment, in gold.

OTHELLO

And once again, thy citizens are safe.
Michael, my arithmetician, count it.

Cassio looks into the chest and counts the sacks of gold.

DUKE

Tis all there.

OTHELLO

I know it is, I trust thee.
Tis Cassio who's the disbeliever.

DUKE

Thou art a noble Venetian citizen.
Yes, thou art a Moor, but thou art not like
other Moors. Venice takes you to its heart.
Thou art known by citizens, our hero.
All of Venice is singing thy praises.
Thou art famous. Tis true, Brabantio?

BRABANTIO

Tis true, M'lord.

OTHELLO

It's not in my nature
to exult myself, but I admit, we
won hard-fought battles.
Is this not a truism, Cassio?

CASSIO

Yes, my General. It is all here, sir.

OTHELLO

Thank you, Cassio. Thank you to the state.
But first, an errand. Please hand me a bag.

Cassio opens the case and takes out a sack of gold and hands it to Othello.

OTHELLO

Take my spoils now to the Sagitary.
Thou hold'st my trust. I must repay a debt.

Cassio exits with the chest of gold.

DUKE

You do us proud, Othello.

BRABANTIO

Is it true thou are a weaver of words?

OTHELLO

Yes, tis true, friend Brabantio, tis true.

BRABANTIO

Can I entice thee to share a meal and
a war story over sumptuous food?

OTHELLO
It has been a long trip, I'd like to rest, sir.

BRABANTIO
In my house lives one of the finest chefs.
Chef Puzo, a meal will he make, that can
tantalize thy palate and sooth thy senses.

OTHELLO
Pasta?

BRABANTIO
Lots of garlic and tomatoes

OTHELLO
Fowl?

BRABANTIO
Freshly plucked, roasted slow and easy.

OTHELLO
Sweets?

BRABANTIO
Marzipan.

OTHELLO
I am your humble guest.

BRABANTIO
Brave Othello, my family, looks forward
to a glorious evening, spent with thee.

DUKE

It is time for thee to relax, Black Moor.

Let Venice lay its treasures at thy feet.

You've earned your reward, make sure he serves meat.

Black Out.

Scene 4

Taverna La Fenice (bar/brothel): Cassio is sitting at a table drinking. Iago enters.

IAGO
So, Michael Cassio, where is the Moor?

CASSIO
Going to repay a debt, friend Iago,
I think he's cuckolding some soldiers' wife.

IAGO
Why dost thou say that?

CASSIO
I took his gold to the Sagitary.
He filched a bag before I left.
Tis a rumor his passion satisfies
the wife of one of his men frequently.
When he gives her his pride, maybe coin too.
He is generous and gives her his gold.

IAGO
Friend, tis much too complicated for me.
I'm thirsty, how does that drink taste to thee?

CASSIO
Good, Iago, taste like I need another.

Iago signals for a drink. Bianca enters. She is wearing a pearl necklace and pearl bracelets. She has a jug of wine and a goblet. She pours Iago a goblet of wine.

IAGO

Girl, I will have whatever he is drinking.

CASSIO

The Moor must choose another Lieutenant?

Bianca refills Cassio's goblet.

IAGO

I heard. Poor Fabriccio, dead and gone.
A good soldier and a better cook.
We will never eat like that, next campaign.

CASSIO

To Fabriccio. A gentleman and
great soldier, a lieutenant to be missed.

They toast and drink.

IAGO

So may Othello make a worthy choice.

They drink again.

IAGO

I hate women.

Bianca exits.

CASSIO

All women or just some?

IAGO

Just wives.

CASSIO

Thankfully, I do not fight that battle.

IAGO

Someday you will.

CASSIO

Maybe. So tell me, Iago…
what are the benefits of marriage?

IAGO

I can name two. If she can cook…a meal.
If a lover…a pleasant time in bed.

CASSIO

There are negatives. For a married man.
First of all, a husband can be cuckold.

IAGO

Do you want to know what is the great lie?

CASSIO

Tell me.

IAGO

Find the right woman, marry her for love,
you will live happily ever after.

CASSIO

Are you not happily living after?

IAGO

I am living the lie. The great white lie.
Saw my wife today, she says she loves me…
but I find my primary needs do not
supersede her secondary needs.
So this poor fool is forced to compromise.
I am forced to sustain my life to her
ultimate will. O, yes, I could fight back,
but I then face the wrath of a mad wife.
Why should I play the fool in this marriage,
when I could easily play my own King?
Then take what I want, yes? When I want it.
I find more and more that compromise of
being nice yields no benefits. So why
should I not look to darker solutions.
Damn God. Damn wives. Damn whatever may come.
My wife makes me so mad, I could kill her.

CASSIO

You, Iago, are a nice fellow. Too nice.

IAGO

I don't want to be seen as a nice guy.
I am a Venetian soldier, my friend.

CASSIO

Relax, Iago, relax. Just enjoy it.
Thou art fair, honest, and forthright.
Everyone likes thee. Thou hast a sparkling
clean reputation, but as a soldier,
thou dost not have the villainous instinct.
Good Iago. Nice Iago, let other men
praise thee for all your sincere qualities.
Enjoy thy repute. Tis the only thing
worth any value in a man's lifetime.

IAGO

Do nice fellows get promoted? No, they don't.
They get passed over. Do wives heed the words
of nice fellows…no. They do what they want?
If a race is run, nice fellows never
finish first. Nice fellows always finish…

CASSIO

Don't say it…

IAGO

Last. So tell me, Cassio
what's the value of being a nice fellow?
What is it worth? And how does life reward
solid ineffectual pleasantry?
Why not at all. I have seen villainous
men rise to power. Covet that power,
spit on peasants, and receive not a whit
of justice. So when niceness is sown, what
is the harvest? Is it a waste of time?
When the race is done, who wins? Not nice guys.

Bianca re-enters. She dusts a chair.

CASSIO

Iago, you have a sharp mind 'tis true.
I see a gentle soul, but my words blur.
Time for me to stop, time to take action.
I have silver in my purse, ambition
on my shoulders, desire in my pants.
The time has come for me to feed the monkey.
Girl, come here.

BIANCA

Who sir? Me sir?

CASSIO

What's thy name?

BIANCA

Would you have my name, sir? Or something else?

CASSIO

I would have more than thy name…and I am
willing to pay at fair market value.

BIANCA

Fair to you, sir. But is it fair to me?

CASSIO

Thou art beautiful. Girl, I'll pay thee this…
just for the sound of thy name, in my ear.

He opens his purse and holds up one silver coin.

BIANCA

The weight of my name is better counted
in gold than silver. Double it, kind sir,
I promise to give, better than my name.

He doubles it.

CASSIO

I have come from the wars and my silver
is my own. O, whisper it loud and clear.

She bites the coin.

BIANCA

My mother named me "Precious Starlight in

the Sky." My friends call me "Heaven and Earth."
But you, sweet sir, can call me Bianca.

CASSIO

A lovelier name never graced a face.
May I go with thee, precious Bianca?

BIANCA

O, there are more things in "Heaven and Earth,"
than are dreamt of in your carnal desires.
Honest question, do you have more silver?

He puts more coins on the table. She scoops up the coins and bites another coin.

BIANCA

Oh, that this too, too solid coin should melt,
Thaw, and resolve itself when tis due.

She takes Cassio by the hand and leads him out.

BIANCA

O yes, let us see what mischief this buys?

IAGO

What he pays for, I should have at home for free.

Roderigo enters with a goblet and a jug. He sits next to Iago. He looks into Iago's mug.

RODERIGO

Is that half empty or 'tis it half full?

IAGO

Empty.

SHAKESPEARE OVER MY SHOULDER TRILOGY

RODERIGO

Let me fill it.

IAGO

Thank you, kind sir.

RODERIGO

Thou hast a nice face, may I ask a question?

IAGO *(aside)*

My day is quickly turning into a
disappointment. Why of course you can ask
I will give an honest answer, not nice.
No matter whose feelings I seem to hurt.

RODERIGO

Are you married?

IAGO

Sometimes, I think I am.
(aside) O, I hurt myself on this repartee.

RODERIGO

Excellent. Friend. I could use some advice.

IAGO

So thou would take advice from a stranger?

RODERIGO

I take advice from a married stranger.

IAGO

I am a stranger in my own marriage,
so I am not sure my advice can help you.
(aside) Once again, I strike myself, I should stop.

RODERIGO

Let me weigh your answer, so I may make
an informed decision. Think'st thou this fair?

IAGO

Trust me stranger, I'm not the man for thee.

RODERIGO

If thou call me Roderigo, we would
no longer be strangers. I am filling
your cup with more wine. Surely a minute
of your time is not too much to ask.

IAGO

Roderigo, I'm a future lieutenant
in Othello's army. For now you can
call me Iago, and if we meet again
then, please call me Lieutenant Iago.

RODERIGO

Iago, I am in love with a pretty maiden.
I want to marry, but she refuses.

IAGO

She has another man?

RODERIGO

No. Free and clear.

IAGO

Her family waits for a man of great wealth.

RODERIGO

My family is wealthy. I have money.

I would lay the treasures of my family
at her feet and so worship her daily.

IAGO

(aside) Man with money, I smell profit in this.
Art thou literate?

Roderigo nods yes.

IAGO

Art thou musical?

Roderigo nods again.

IAGO

Problem solved, but the answer is not free.
If given free thou wilt not value it,
coin makes it worthy of considering.

RODERIGO

I am anxious to hear. Friend, for thy purse.

Roderigo puts coins on the table.

IAGO

Write her songs of love. Thou art musical.

RODERIGO

I am no musician…but I've got rhythm.

IAGO

Well, friend Roderigo, there thou hast it.
An easy answer. Sing to her. Win her
with thy voice. Better still, write her a song.

RODERIGO
Yes. A song. Of course. She will love my voice.
My mother does. I often sing to her.

IAGO
Roderigo, hire some musicians.
Let the sincerity of thy voice win her.
She cannot but fall in love with true style
once thou caress the subtle phrases of
a song penned by thee, sung in thine own voice.
Dost, thou know the song, *Love is a wet dream?*

RODERIGO
Yes, of course.

IAGO
Let me hear thy baritone.
I want to judge the extent of thy talent.

RODERIGO
I have a better song. It is English
A soldier's song. I think you will like it.

Roderigo sings.

And let me the canakin clink, clink.
And let me the canakin clink.
A soldier's a man
O, man's life but a span,
Why then let a soldier drink.
O, yes, let a soldier drink.

IAGO
O, Roderigo, that was…perfection.
Thou hast a golden throat, my eager friend.

Superb, thou should be on stage in Rome.
"O Thespians of Italy beware."

RODERIGO

Thou really think'st so?

IAGO

As I am honest.
I have ne'er in my life heard such a sound.

RODERIGO

I've always sung in the house for Mother.
She swears I have the most pleasing voice.

IAGO

(aside) Does a mother's love know no bounds? "Pleasing?"
Not just pleasing, magnificent, 'tis true.
I will tell thee this, Young Roderigo,
I wish I could be there to see her face
when thou woos her with thy sweet melodies.

RODERIGO

Thou hast given me the courage to try.

IAGO

Do not try Roderigo…please, just do.
You will succeed, and strong love will enter.

RODERIGO

I go. Determined to secure my love.

Roderigo exits singing.

IAGO

May all blessings be upon thee, my friend.
Simpleton. Goddamn, that was too easy.
I will blame this encounter on his youth.
They can't all be this easy. Or could they?
Being a bad man has some advantages.
Granted this is just a first step, e'en so.
My steps will get surer as I go along.
A good villain should walk before he runs.
God, how I wish I were the lieutenant,
I could practice on all the service men,
high and low, arrogant officers and
simple infantrymen, the calvary,
cannon men. Cooks, spear chuckers. I would have
my own endless supply of simpletons
to choose from. I run ahead of myself,
the Moor must first choose me. Who else has the
wherewithal to command men such as myself?
Michael Cassio? Why, certainly not.
He lives in numbers; I live in battle.
O, yes, modestly I must claim, no one.
It will come ere rise of a foreign sun.

Black Out.

ACT II

Scene 1

Casa di Iago: Othello enters.

OTHELLO
What ho! Is anyone at home? Iago?

Emilia rushes into the room. She is dressed in her finest dress, showing plenty of cleavage.

EMILIA
I was preparing to come visit thee.

OTHELLO
Yes, I can see that. That dress is lovely.

She kisses him. He does not respond and pushes her away.

OTHELLO
Thy husband is gone?

EMILIA
Out drinking, I think.

OTHELLO
Sad news, have I?

EMILIA
Come, we don't have much time.

She kisses him again, and he breaks the kiss.

OTHELLO
Emilia, we must stop this madness.

EMILIA
While you were away, all I thought was of thee, us.
Your black stallion astride my white mare.

OTHELLO
I cannot. I've had a revelation.

EMILIA
Why? What is this? Thou knowest I love thee.

OTHELLO
It is time we each seek a brand-new day.
I bring this gift for thee, Emilia.
For time we have shared and to help thee.

Othello brings out a sack of gold to give to her.

EMILIA
I am not a whore! I give what I want
from my heart. O, you so do wound me, Moor.
Think you, what we shared, I shared for profit?
I prize you. I dance for your melody.
I dance for your pleasure and our delight.
I do not crave nor I want your silver.

OTHELLO
Tis not silver, Emilia, tis gold.

EMILIA

Think'st thou my passion can be bought like some
common strumpet? I say, not so, black man.
I give from my heart. Heart to heart, I share.
We sing as one. We love as one, not gold.

OTHELLO

No, Emilia, I say, we are no more.
I have sinned. Know this, I will sin no more.

EMILIA

Othello, please let this be one more time.

OTHELLO

I cannot.

EMILIA

O, let this be the last time.
Let me savor this final time. Let my
thoughts know peace since no longer are we one.

OTHELLO

Thou hast many memories of us.

EMILIA

Just seventeen. Make it at least twenty.

OTHELLO

I cannot. For thine husband is honest,
my true ancient, mark you, a good soldier.
This is a mistake that keeps on growing.
And we must stop, so it grows no further.
I want to make thy husband lieutenant.
A worthy commission for valued skills.

EMILIA

I know he sends three mediators to
sue for your approval, is that not wise?

OTHELLO

If I make him my lieutenant, you'll stop.
Can you hold your emotions, Emilia?

EMILIA

O, why should I, Othello? Think of it,
we would be closer, and excuses would
not have to be dreamed up or invented.

OTHELLO

'Tis so, not the words I wanted to hear.

EMILIA

Did I not please thee?

OTHELLO

Yes. Thou art skillful.
But I should have stopped long before now.

EMILIA

And was I not pliable to thy will?

OTHELLO

Thou made me very happy, Lady E.

EMILIA

Then grant me one last boon. Love me like you
are going off to war, ne'er to return.
One final kiss. Black Moor. One final thrust.

OTHELLO

So you would cuckold your husband again?

EMILIA

Tis small vice. Is it sport? Yes, I think so.
Have we not affections? Desire for
this sport, and frailty as man might have?
The ills we do, their ills instruct us so.

OTHELLO

No. This ends now. Iago is a good man.
I do repent that I let my lust get
the better of me. My good sense failed me.

EMILIA

During war, did my husband abstain?

OTHELLO

I know not.

EMILIA

Othello, I know my husband.
In some battles, were there women about?
For know this, Moor, I know my husband's heart.
Nay the heart of most men, thine included.
You men cannot resist a sassy girl
or a conquered soul. It is not thy fault
it is my husband's. I would never let
thee pick my plum had I not known Iago
has tasted foreign fruit. You men think you
are the only ones with an appetite.
I am sure thee hast conquered cities and
availed thyself of fresh defeated spoils.
Iago is not special in that regard.

Can thou honestly tell me he hasn't
supped at foreign tables? Eaten their fruit?
Well, I have an appetite. I have thirst.
Thou quench all my desires. Yes, you, Moor.

OTHELLO
Understand thy logic. Truly I do.
But I must make a new start for my soul.
I don't want to soil my approach this life.
On my knees, I have prayed to my Allah.
I have repented my previous ways.
No, my heart is following a new quest.
There is a special gift awaiting me,
but I must walk the road to righteousness.
So I follow the path of abstinence.
I follow the path of obedience.

EMILIA
Tomorrow. Begin tomorrow. Not today.
Let us share one final time, united.

OTHELLO
Emilia, it does not work that way.
The start of tomorrow begins today.

Black Out.

Scene 2

Casa Di Brabantio: Roderigo strums his mandolin. Brabantio is holding a book.

RODERIGO

Senator, this is one of the finest
mandolins in all of great Italy.
I pray you listen with your cultured ear.

BRABANTIO

O, Roderigo, no time have I to
enjoy your sycophancy this evening.

RODERIGO

Dear Senator, my appearance I will
promptly let you know. I have come to sing
to your daughter.

BRABANTIO

Tonight? Please not tonight.
O, Roderigo, not now. Not tonight.
Tonight is not a good night.

RODERIGO *(sings)*

You always says that!

BRABANTIO

Still you miss the point.
I repeat those words so often because

thou hast no sense of time or decorum.
When will thou comprehend my daughter is
not for thee?

RODERIGO
Future Father, just give me
a chance, thou will see my strong qualities.

BRABANTIO
Roderigo, I see your strong qualities,
that's why I don't want you here.

RODERIGO
I have qualities yet undiscovered.

BRABANTIO
Being able to bore citizens is
not an admirable quality, boy.
You must leave, Roderigo. I have a
dinner guest soon to arrive. So be gone.

RODERIGO *(sings)*
Thou aren't inviting me to sup with thee?

BRABANTIO
Be gone! Does that sound like an invitation?
Ciao, Arriverderci, dost understand?
Adieu, au revoir, bon voyage, mon ami,
Adios, senor. Get on thy horse and ride.
Thou profess to be educated man.
So tell me, which language is thy strongest?
Tis not Italian. Nor any other.

RODERIGO *(laughs)*
Aren't thou inviting me to sup with thee?

BRABANTIO

Roderigo, I am inviting thee
to leave ere my anger find a target.

RODERIGO

I must go?

BRABANTIO

Go!

RODERIGO

But before I leave thee.
I have a present for Desdemona.

BRABANTIO

Saints above. I endure idiocy.

RODERIGO

After my song, I present a present.
A gift of quality, this pearl necklace.

He shows Brabantio a pearl necklace.

RODERIGO *(sings)*

She'd be the perfect pale pearl of my life.

BRABANTIO

Keep thy song, keep thy fine white pearls, young man.
Keep thy dreams to yourself. When thou see'st
my perfectly placed dwelling, keep walking.

RODERIGO

Brabantio, What? No, sense of romance?
Dost thou not remember when thou were young
and in love?

BRABANTIO

I do. I did it better.
Now, leave, go. Young man go. I say be gone.

Othello enters.

OTHELLO

Brabantio, good evening, my friend.
And who is this?

BRABANTIO

No one. Please, Othello, enter my home,
I will be with thee soon. Go, go, inside.

Othello enters Brabantio's home.

RODERIGO

He is thy dinner guest?

BRABANTIO

Yes! Now please go!

RODERIGO *(whispers)*

Brabantio, did thou notice he's black?

BRABANTIO

As a midnight sky. Yes, I am not blind.
Go, young man, before you raise my ire.

RODERIGO

Thou art sitting at a table to dine
with a Moor. A black man, and not with me?

BRABANTIO

Roderigo, thou art living in Venice.
We are a progressive city, my friend.
We have many foreigners living here.
The waterways bring travelers from all
over the world. Othello is a man,
a warrior, a soldier, a hero
of the wars. Thou should respect a man who
puts his life in front of an enemy
to protect thee and me and all other
Christians. I can see thou think'st because thou
has grown up with privilege thou should'st be more
entitled to things you want. What bothers
me is my daughter is part of thy list.
Poor little man, we must learn to grow as
human beings. I want thee to leave and
think of how thy small mind misjudged a man.

RODERIGO

I go, old man, but beware, the time will come,
when you see that Moor as just a black bum.

Black Out.

Scene 3

Casa Di Brabantio: Brabantio and Othello are laughing over a story. Brabantio points to Othello's dagger. Othello smiles and draws his dagger, then hands it to Brabantio. Othello wipes his beard with his handkerchief. It is spotted with strawberries.

OTHELLO
The blade of this dagger is one of three
shards that was once a sword called *Durenda*.

Desdemona peeks into the room. Othello sees her, and she scurries away.

OTHELLO
For *Durenda* was broken on a stone
in three parts, so the song of the sword could
sing no more. The sacred sword belonged
to a Paladin named Roland. He had
fought for King Charles of Spain during the time
of Charlemagne. Reigns an old legend that
the soldier who carries this dagger of
Durenda cannot be killed in battle,
But when the Day of Atonement arrives
t'will die by his own hand using this blade.

BRABANTIO
Is't even so? O, tis a wonderment!

OTHELLO

Tis but an old crone's tale. A witch's brew.

Desdemona enters with a note.

DESDEMONA

Father, here is a message from the Duke.

BRABANTIO

Thank you, daughter. See to our guest's dessert.

DESDEMONA

So you like marzipan?

OTHELLO

Sweet and lovely.

Desdemona exits.

BRABANTIO

Friend, Othello, I am called by the Duke.
No, stay. Please enjoy your dessert, eat up.

Othello rises to leave. Brabantio insists that Othello stay. Brabantio exits as Desdemona returns with marzipan.

OTHELLO

I saw you listening.

DESDEMONA

I'm sorry. I did not hear the story
from the beginning.

OTHELLO

I can start again.

DESDEMONA

O, no. Those stories were for my father.
Dost thou have a tale that can be mine?

OTHELLO

I could weave you a tale that would make thy
heart shutter, make thine eyes dance in glory.

DESDEMONA

Please do. But will it be a tale just for me?

OTHELLOA

I will weave thee a story, never heard.

He taps a chair for her to sit and join him. She crosses and sits.

DESDEMONA

A secret story?

OTHELLO

No one lives to contradict my story.
These words have never passed lips to explain
my adventure. Would it please thee to hear?

DESDEMONA

T'would please me to touch thee. Touching thy hair.

OTHELLO

Then, come here, Chuck, and give me thine hand.

*He takes her hand, kisses it, and puts it on his head. He is wearing a keffiyeh,
a head scarf. She slowly takes it off. It is a sensual move. He is wearing a
taqiyah, a skull cap; she removes it and touches his hair.*

DESDEMONA

Soft, so soft. I wondered how this would feel.

He strokes her other hand.

OTHELLO

Smooth as monumental alabaster.

DESDEMONA

Thank you, Othello. T'was very kind, sir.

OTHELLO

Say that again.

DESDEMONA

What?

OTHELLO

My name.

DESDEMONA

Othello?

OTHELLO

The sound of my name rolling from thine lips
feels of a breeze on a wet afternoon
in Damascus. Say it again, sweet girl.

DESDEMONA

Othello. *(She giggles.)* So that is pleasing to thee?

OTHELLO

Very. Thou Christian dream of an ideal woman.

DESDEMONA
I hope not just Christian.

OTHELLO
Lovely Desdemona, I will tell thee
of an adventure, I experienced
as a child, in the city of Aleppo.
T'was a time, I had to learn the ways of
foreign lands. And Aleppo t'was thriving.
Lots of Chinese merchants, Jewish scholars,
Syrian soldiers, Spanish sailors, and
religious sages. As a cabin boy,
I filled my nights and days on a ship called,
The Dove. We would sail from port to port.
Dropping off sweet spices or picking up
expensive textiles of cotton or silks.
Once my captain, a big bear of a man,
Saladin, for he was named after the
great Muslim warrior, instructed me
to prepare his cabin as he left to
enjoy his evening. My duty was
simple, clean his cabin. Make sure that his
Akshaya silver bowl was polished and
ready to cleanse his face on his return.
See that his bed had fresh Asian silk sheets.
I made sure all the gold and silver in
his cabin shine like the buckle of a
Prussian scabbard. After I finished my
work, I would nest at the foot of his bed.
At night, I was used as his foot warmer.
He was known to keep valuable things in
his cabin, gold, silver, and Othello.
No one dare thought of theft. His temper fierce,
Saladin had once been a warrior,
but he had enemies, from España.

One cold wintry night, ere his return, I
felt a calloused hand cover my mouth and
snatch me from my favorite sleeping spot.
The hand belonged to a Spanish sailor.
I bit that hand, for it did not belong
to the hand that was feeding me. I saw
Three Spaniards ransacking my master's cabin.
They had come to steal cargo, but we had
unloaded the ship, the only thing of
value was found in the captain's cabin.
They chased me around that cabin, trying
to subdue me, but I was quick, agile,
determined, and feisty. I jumped over
the bed, climbed the wall, threw gold cups, silver
bowls at them. It was a most deadly chase.

DESDEMONA

Did you escape?

OTHELLO

Before Saladin's return,
the Spaniards took all the gold and silver
from the cabin, stole me, and threw me on
a slave ship. Bound for South America.
I was dropped into a cargo hole with
some wretched black souls. Men, women, and me.
It was filthy. Excrement was everywhere,
the true smell of urine. Men sat in vomit.
For a boy of ten, t'was a scary sight.
I did not see the sun till we landed
on the shores of LeFrance Antarctique.
I was put up for auction on the block.

DESDEMONA

'Tis Strange.

179

OTHELLO

Cruel men stuck dirty fingers in my mouth
to look at my teeth and stripped me naked.
Eventually, I was sold to a man
named Nicolas Villegagnon. I did
not know white men could be so cruel
to other men and little boys. Simply
'cause one man's skin is dark, the other's not.

DESDEMONA

'Tis passing strange.

OTHELLO

I watched this man Nicolas and took note
of his habits, desires, whims, and tastes.
He was rich, arrogant, privileged, and cruel.
I watched him handle men, friends, and his foes.
I saw him torture enemies and praise
the torturer. I wanted to escape.

DESDEMONA

'Tis pitiful.

OTHELLO

Watching this man, I soon learned his weaknesses.
I would use those to try for my escape.

DESDEMONA

'Tis wondrous pitiful.

OTHELLO

He loved drink…and drink is a provoker of three things.

DESDEMONA

What three things does drink provoke?

OTHELLO

Bravery, sleep, and urine.

DESDEMONA

Is it true?

OTHELLO

A little drink makes a quiet man brave,
loud, and fearless. Not enough drink causes a man
to urinate and maybe want more drink.
Just enough drink puts a man away with
sound sleep. Didn't want him brave nor pissing.
Wanted him asleep.

DESDEMONA

And that is what you did?
Thou got him drunk, he would sleep through the night.

OTHELLO

No. I hit him in the head with a mallet
and escaped without a fight.

DESDEMONA

Did he die?

OTHELLO

I do not know, Desdemona. For I ne'er
returned nor spoke it, from that day to this.

DESDEMONA

O, thou hast grown from a strong little boy
into a brave warrior Othello.
Thou art a great soldier. Oh, I wish I
had not heard these stories, yet I wish that

God had made me such a man, as thou art.
For thou art truly a big, brave, black Moor.

OTHELLO
Young, beautiful, Pearl. T'will be many
eager Italians knockin' at thy door.

DESDEMONA
Thank thee for thy sweet words…but I'm not sure.
If thou has a friend that might love a girl
like me, thou should teach him how to tell thy
story, and Othello that would woo me.

OTHELLO
My, my! Woulds't thou marry such a fellow?

DESDEMONA
No man such as thee ever crossed my door.
It is why I was not in love before.

OTHELLO
To Allah, I confess love sacked my heart.

DESDEMONA
If you convert, we could marry in a
Catholic wedding. I would be yours, you mine.

OTHELLO
Islam does not forbid me to marry
outside my faith. Allah will bless us.

DESDEMONA
I think of my Father, to marry a
Moor would be hard on him. To marry a
Christian Moor would ease my guilt and his pain.

Convert, I will seal my life with thee and
know my God will bless this holy union.

Othello kisses her hand.

DESDEMONA

Othello, may I touch your hair again?

Othello places her hand on his head. As she leans in to touch his hair, their faces are very close. He kisses her.

OTHELLO

Your eyes are kind, thy lips soft and taste sweet.
A second kiss would make my world complete.

She kisses him.

Black Out.

ACT III
Scene 1

The Plazzo Ducale: Brabantio enters and clears his throat.

DUKE
Brabantio, such a timely response.

BRABANTIO
M'lord, I am at thy service.

DUKE
We've a problem brewing in Cyprus with Yasef Nasi.

BRABANTIO
The Portuguese Jew? What is the matter?

DUKE
His influence on Sultan Salim
is taking a turn, he's more combative.

BRABANTIO
Salim's a drunk. Easily influenced.

DUKE
Military action is an option
but I do not want to disturb the truce.
I don't want Othello back in Cyprus.
He just returned, so I would like to give
him time to rest and recuperate.

BRABANTIO

Let us look dispassionately at the
problem and make an informed decision.

DUKE

Senator that is why I called on thee.
Thou art able to hold thy emotions
to think with a calm, clear mind. An asset.

BRABANTIO

Thank you, Your Grace.

DUKE

Yes, let us look at this
with a dispassionate eye. The facts are,
Yasef Nasi has the Sultan's ear.
We know Venice taxing the Orthodox
Greeks is not beneficial at this time.

BRABANTIO

Gracious Duke, Venice needs the money now.

DUKE

True, Cyprus taxes go to good use here.

BRABANTIO

Our strength is that we know that Nasi will
profit if we continue this fighting.
We must starve that crafty Jew. Starve him fast.
Find a way to get the Sultan talking.
The more he talks, the less time for fighting.

DUKE

I could send an envoy with terms for peace.

BRABANTIO

Do we want peace?

DUKE

O, hell no. we want time.

BRABANTIO

Sultan Salim is a drunk. Send him wine.

DUKE

We could send him fine Italian red wines.

BRABANTIO

Send an envoy with red wines on the new
assumption that we are going to talk peace.
Our negotiator talks in circles,
keep the wine flowing and the goblets filled.

DUKE

We've got to keep Nasi out of the room,
he is a smart Jew. T'will see right through it.

BRABANTIO

What is Nasi's weakness?

DUKE

He's been trying
to resettle Jews in Tiberias.

BRABANTIO

Let your lead negotiator know that.

DUKE

Better more Jews there than to have them here.

BRABANTIO

We want him to think how we understand
the plight of his people. We've sympathy
for all Hebrews. Use, we have Jews living
here in Venice. That can be quite a tool.

DUKE

I don't want to see more Jews migrating
to my city. Enough, we have enough.
I am dealing with conflicts all the time.

BRABANTIO

Better the Jews we know than those unseen.
Too many cultures will make envy green.

Black Out.

Scene 2

Basilica San Marco: Othello enters and sees a priest. The priest has been in the garden and has a basket of flowers.

OTHELLO

Priest, I've questions of faith. Can'st thou answer?

PRIEST

Please, I am called Father Gaetano.
So are you not the hero of Venice?

OTHELLO

Dost thou know me? We have met before? Where?

PRIEST

The Moor of Venice. Othello is known.

OTHELLO

You flatter me, Priest, but I have questions.
I need true answers. Are you a wise man?

PRIEST *(laughs)*

Some say yes, but others would disagree.
Let us look at the subject and maybe
I can offer you solace and comfort.

OTHELLO

I seek to marry.

PRIEST

Admirable…but this
is not a mosque. Consult with your imam?

OTHELLO

An imam in Venice? Hard to find who
will perform a Christian wedding.

PRIEST

I see.

OTHELLO

I am thinking of converting.

PRIEST

I see.
What Christian family are we speaking of?

OTHELLO

Tis a secret. T'will stay that way for now.

PRIEST

A story I would share about secret
weddings? Something I witnessed in my past.

OTHELLO

You're a man of Allah. I will hear you.

PRIEST

In my youth, I was an altar boy for
my church in a town far away from here.
I had a green thumb and often aided
a local friar. He taught me about
herbs and plants, the strength of a wild flower
or the sad weakness of a dying root.

OTHELLO
I listen, Priest, but I hear not a point.

PRIEST
The friar, my mentor, aided a young
lad, just a few years older than myself.
The young man had fallen in love with a
beauty. My friar wed the couple in
secret. The pair had come from two feuding
households both alike in dignity.

OTHELLO
Yet you speak as if it was a problem.

PRIEST
Verona was a small town with many
small minds. This friar had hoped the wedding
would unite families and end the feud.
What should have led to bliss ended tragic.

OTHELLO
Priest, they were children, I am a soldier,
My wedding's a secret, but I promise
thee. My bride's father will know soon after.
Now, Priest, a second question I do have,
I want to know if thou will marry us?

PRIEST
Are you sure 'tis something you want to do?
Becoming a Christian is not a step
to be taken lightly. Do you believe
in Jesus Christ as your Lord and Savior?

OTHELLO
The tenets of Catholicism I

must first try to learn. No Bible I own.
I have only read the Holy Qu'ran.

PRIEST

I see. There is a commitment that is
made when one becomes Catholic, Othello.
'Tis a story in the Holy Bible
Of Abraham sacrificing his son.
His belief was so strong in God that he
was willing to kill his son, an angel
stayed his hand. Do you think you would have that
kind of faith in our Christianity?

OTHELLO

O, Abraham's story is known to me.
'Tis in the Holy Qu'ran. Abraham
was going to sacrifice his son Ishmael
and a heavenly angel stops his hand.

PRIEST

No, Othello, not Ishmael. T'was Isaac.

OTHELLO

No. We Muslims believe it was Ismael.

PRIEST

Holy Bible proclaims his son Isaac. Isaac.

OTHELLO

Ishmael.

PRIEST

Isaac.

OTHELLO

Ishmael.

PRIEST

Isaac!

OTHELLO

If the story is in both Holy books…
is it not then the same Allah or God?

PRIEST

Why, yes. I ne'er thought of it in those terms.
But God and Allah are one in the same?
Would you leave your faith and convert for love?

OTHELLO

I have had all kinds of women. Some I
have taken, for I am a true soldier.
Some have given freely for I am not
unattractive to the opposite sex.
some I have bought, because I've the money,
the time and the need to release desires.
I have lost count of the encounters with girls,
strumpets, captives, widows, ladies, matrons,
and wives, for yes, I have cuckold men's wives.
I have sometimes found wives to be a lot
more satisfying than a courtesan.
Eager to please me and fearless in bed.
High-brow ladies, kitchen maids, young virgins,
and of course, old maids. But now, Christian Priest,
I say this 'cause I have come to my end.

PRIEST

You have found love. Christian love.
So you would marry this Christian woman?

OTHELLO

We want to marry. She will not marry
if I'm not Christian. Can you convert me?

PRIEST

Yes.

OTHELLO

And wed me to a Christian lady?

PRIEST

Yes, my black friend, convert you and wed you
to your love, If that, you so desire.

OTHELLO

Tis not an easy choice, I must wrestle
with my heart and wrestle with Aqeedah.
I shall return.

PRIEST

What is the lady's name?

OTHELLO

Priest, in good time. You will not only learn
her name, but you will meet her face to face.
And these church walls may be my wedding place.

Othello exits.

PRIEST

So the Moor wants to become a Christian.
He wants to embrace Jesus Christ. So he
can honestly embrace his white woman.
I am obligated by the tenants
of my faith to welcome this Moor to Christ.

I don't like it. But what choice have I, now?
A hero he is. So I must serve him.
I lay this dilemma at the feet of
this infatuated, dull, silly girl.
Had I gotten her family name I could
stop this travesty. This damn sacrilege.
If he had not fallen in love, I would
not be in this sinful predicament.
Will he turn his back on Islam? Will he
be seduced by one of our white women?
I conclude he'll need to wed in secret.
This Blackamoor will want to worship.
He must, then, find a church to pray to God.
My God, not his Allah. He is ruled by
his carnal desires. He thinks changing
faith will bless this Goddamn fornication.
T'will be my church he comes to for worship.
It will be my church as I am the Priest
who brought him to Christ. All Venice will know.
A black man sitting in my church, kneeling
in my pews. For my parishioners, this
does not bode well. My worshipers seeing
an ink spot on white paper. I will lose
the more ardent followers. Word will spread
that the Black Moor comes to my church. Monkey!
I'll be the laughing stock of other priests.
Bishops will know me and snicker, tis so.
Zounds, but what am I now? Anonymous,
this too is true. But with this black Moor in
attendance, lofty cardinals, bishops,
jealous priests will soon know and learn my name.
This cathedral will become famous for
having that black heathen ape sitting here
among my clean white Christians. I will be
famous as the child of God who brought this

heathen to the bosom of our Christ.
Other priests will look at me with envy.
So becoming bishop could rise sooner.
Being cardinal will be within my grasp.
From there, who knows. The priest with the black man
in his congregation. This has promise.
All of Venice knows his name. Will it not
be the same for me? In a field with white
congregations, white priests, white cathedrals,
I alone will stand separate from the crowd.
I will have converted a Muslim to Christ.
Thank you, Jesus, for showing me the way,
This light that shines is opportunity.
Good book says, "I was blind, but now I see."

Black Out.

Scene 3

Casa Di Cassio: Cassio is sitting at a table solving a math problem with an abacus.

CASSIO

Now is the autumn of my malcontent,
which bleeds in the winter of ambition.
Soldiers striving for their recognition.
Lieutenant's promotion, 'tis such a farce,
seeking advancement to incompetence.
I know my limitations, its numbers.
I rise in comfort to the blessed mark
of my capabilities. Numbers dance
on paper for me. Their cold hard truth is
a revelation. I know what best suits
a situation. Numbers never lie,
never deceive, nor do they change their sums.
When all else fails, I can count on the truth
of mathematics. Like an abacus from
the Chinese, I shift numbers with ease.
The complexity of life. Let others
strive for more, I am satisfied with less.

Othello enters. He is holding a letter.

OTHELLO

What ho, Cassio!

CASSIO

General, a surprise? Good to see you.
So what brings thee to my humble dwelling?

OTHELLO

Michael Cassio, I must talk to thee.

CASSIO

Othello, sir, so please you, I am yours.

OTHELLO

I need a favor, such a deed will be
rewarded. Deliver this letter to
Brabantio's daughter, the fair young girl
he calls Desdemona. Can thou do that?
I think it a prudent step for me, friend,
It must be someone other than myself.

Cassio takes the letter.

CASSIO

I am happy to assist in any
and all endeavors. For her eyes only.

Othello starts to leave, then stops. He thinks then…

OTHELLO

Michael Cassio!
Thou knowest Frabriccio is now gone?

CASSIO

Tragic ending, sir. Fabriccio had
The respect of his men. Of their hearts and
their bellies. His Sunday night company
meals were such a gastronomic delight.

OTHELLO

I will miss him.

CASSIO

A talented soldier.

OTHELLO

I needs must replace him with a good man.

CASSIO

Who are your choices, sir? Please share your list.

OTHELLO

A soldier with a good reputation.
A good reputation carries strong weight.

CASSIO

Do I know this choice?

OTHELLO

Yes, intimately.
Michael Cassio, you're my lieutenant.

CASSIO

O, General, I'm not the proper choice.
My field experience is limited.

OTHELLO

Soldier, do you question your general?
I am not asking for thy permission.
You have no say. I command. You follow.
Think thou because I am black, I lack knowledge?
Do not raise my anger, young Florentine.
For my ill temper will give way to wrath.

CASSIO
But, sir, am I...? Are you? I do not think...

OTHELLO
Silence! Think not. I give thee a gift so
many men would die for. I raise your rank
with certainty that you can fulfill all
it demands Do not question. Don't waiver.
Do not dare to think me unwise in my
choice. There are half a dozen soldiers that
covet this prize. I know their value, as
I do know yours. Being lieutenant will
raise their status in Venice and the world.
It will afford opportunity for
a common man to stand in a room with
elite minds. Think you not some peasant would
like to kiss the King's ring? I say yea, son.
And lose an eye tooth for the privilege.

Othello wipes his brow with his handkerchief.

OTHELLO
There is something I see in thee, that thou
cannot see in thyself. This is not a
debate, young Cassio. The commission
is yours, and I am correct in my choice.

CASSIO
Yes. Yes, my General. I do accept.

OTHELLO
Good. T'will make arrangements, young Cassio.
thou hast a sterling reputation with
the men, they will be as happy to hear
this good news, as I am to tell it.

Iago enters.

IAGO
What ho, Cassio, are you ready
to join me for a night of revelry?

OTHELLO
My ancient Iago, do thou and this my
new lieutenant go out to share the night?

IAGO
New lieutenant? Cassio? Tis a joke?

CASSIO
Iago, I have cause for celebration.
Let us drink, be merry and watch the sun
rise on a new day. I am overjoyed.

IAGO
My friend, I can see thou art serious.

OTHELLO
I've made him my new lieutenant, Iago.
Replacing Fabriccio as of now.

IAGO
I'm truly flabbergasted.

CASSIO
As am I.

OTHELLO
Soldiers, I leave you to your revelry.

Othello exits.

IAGO

Well, friend Cassio, It looks like we have
great cause for songs, drink, and celebration.

CASSIO

T'was greatly surprised. I thought the gen'ral
would pick someone like you. I complain not,
I will gladly take this advance, for it
increases my purse, my place in the world.
I never dreamed of such riches as these.

IAGO

Come let us go and celebrate. Tonight, I shall
treat you, tomorrow you can afford
to buy me dinner and expensive wine.

They exit. As they leave, Bianca enters. She watches them go.

BIANCA

Michael Cassio has been given
a commission. He's a worthy man.
A man of strong and high reputation.
Maybe it is time for him to marry?
Maybe it is time for me to marry?
Why should I spend my life chasing ducats?
One day, I will be old, and that race will
be harder to win. I should find a man
now and settle down. My problem is I
have larceny in my heart and only
the golden coin can satisfy that itch.
O, can I let my heart's thievery go?
He's not bright, although he's good with numbers.
I must weigh the evidence for making

a husband from a respectable man.
Yes, Michael Cassio is such a man.
And yes, he would make a worthy husband.
But can I control him? Yes, I think so.
I cannot be a strumpet my whole life.
I have other attributes, besides my
talent in bed. I can cook, I can sew.
But marriage is such a puzzle to me.
'Tis easy to control men who buy you.
Money is tangible, but when a man
loves you, a woman must be careful on
how she achieves her goals.
Money on the table solves most problems.
My problem, he knows I am a strumpet.
He's paid for me. More than once. He has hunger.
Will he eat a dish already tasted?
Cassio knows I am good in his bed.
He should want to know my mind. But what man
truly knows his wife's mind? Easy answer,
none. Cassio has tasted fruit of my loins,
but would he want to win and love my heart?
I needs must hold my contempt inside till
the trap has been sprung. Patience is the key.
Bianca must take what God has laid in
her path. I will marry this man, for sure.
The only question how best to achieve it.
He loves my body, there is no question,
even so, he must learn to love my mind.
O, marriage is my problem's solution.
So t'will be my goal and resolution.

Black Out.

Scene 4

Casa Di Othello: He kneels on his prayer rug.

OTHELLO
Now, must I ask in my prayers for guidance,
and I pray to Allah for clarity.

Basilica San Marco: The priest kneels in prayer.

PRIEST
If the Moor chooses Christianity.
I am God's vessel, his salvation.
This be a test from God for my white soul,
to bring this black man to the holy Christ.
I must be strong enough to endure the
consequences. I must pray for guidance.

Casa Di Iago: Iago enters.

IAGO
Cassio spreads rumors of Othello
cuckolding soldiers' wives. Rumors that the
lusty Moor exchanges gold and receives
female favors, sacks of pure gold.

Iago tosses a sack of gold on the floor.

IAGO

Maybe the Moor hath leaped into my seat.
for this sack of gold, I found hidden in
my home. Two years away I am, two years
is not enough time for her this wealth to
accumulate, honestly. 'Tis most foul.
Me thinks, my soul has been abused. Most foul,
indeed. And Cassio spreads his pride as
he rides the unicorn of ambition.
No chance have I for lieutenant, nor any
of the garlands that might grace those profits.
I stand here a cuckold husband, bereft
of my true station in life. I should be
an officer! I seek revenge. I pray
for a light to mete out my next course of
action. O, dear God, how might I see my
enemies fall? Shine your bright light on me.

Iago kneels and prays.

Casa Di Brabantio. Desdemona enters.

DESDEMONA

I love the Moor. All of his qualities.
He fills my dreams and all my desires.
Leaving home will not be an easy task.
My father is a strong, determined man,
but would he oppose and try to defeat
such a man as Othello and succeed?
I think not. Those other suitors that cry
and profess their love for me are mere boys.
My father would crush them, confuse them, and
control them. I do not think that will be

so with my Othello. I will be free
to live my own life. To love my own way.
No longer under thumbs of paternal
demands. I will become a full-fledged woman in
the arms of this black man. I pray to God,
and I thank him for bringing me a man.
For bringing Othello into my life.

Casa Di Othello: Othello is praying.

OTHELLO

I pray to Allah for guidance. But if
Jehovah is God and God is Allah,
all paths lead to the one God. The same God.
I think I'm having an epiphany.
Wisdom is given to me by Allah.
For wanting to fill my desire of
the beautiful, saintly Desdemona.
As my prayers go up from this holy ground,
I look to heaven and blessings come down.

Black Out.

House lights up: A lady in waiting crosses to center stage.

LADY MARY

If we shadows have offended,
think but this and all is mended.
Relieve your bladders,
that's all that matters.
Stretch your legs, walk don't run
return in ten, you should be done.

END OF THE FIRST HALF (Intermission)

ACT IV

Scene 1

Taverna La Felice: Iago and Cassio are having a drink at the bar and laughing.

IAGO
Another drink, Lieutenant?

CASSIO
Iago, dost thou laugh at my expense?

IAGO
No, sir, for surety, I call you, sir.
We are celebrating Othello's choice.

CASSIO
Yes, we are.

IAGO
A fine choice.

CASSIO
I think 'tis true.

IAGO
But why? So, why do you think he chose you?

CASSIO
I know not, friend. He sees something in me.

IAGO

As do I, but soldiering isn't it.
No offense to thee, Michael Cassio.
Thou art great with numbers. Thou knows how to
move supplies, but hand to hand combat you
do not excel. Thou knows this to be true.

CASSIO

Iago, I complain not about my
promotion. Othello is a wise
general. Who knows his plans for me?
I am not going to stop living up to
his expectations. Ere I lose his trust.

IAGO

Well said, Michael Cassio, tis, well said.
Not unlike a sycophant to say this.

CASSIO

Your honesty is refreshing, Iago.

IAGO

Clearly, you will not be my sycophant.

CASSIO

He's our general. We're all sycophants,
to him. It's also called following orders, sir.
You talk as if you thought the commission
should go to you. Are you a jealous man?

IAGO

Jealous? No! I like being an ancient.
No one does my job, friend, better than me.
The Moor knows that. I am valuable to
him in my present station, I think you

know that, Cassio. I'm happy for thee.
To prove my love for thee, let me buy you
another drink.

CASSIO

Thank you, honest Iago.
Truly, thou art a man of integrity.

Bianca enters.

IAGO

If I looked for a leader, I could not
find a better lieutenant or nobler
soldier than one Michael Cassio.

BIANCA

Michael, art thou relaxed and comfortable?

CASSIO

Bianca, one more drink and I will be
a totally new man. I have news for
thee, I have been promoted by the Moor.

BIANCA

Tell me about it.

IAGO

I now must go, friend.

CASSIO

No, Iago, stay, hear me tell the tale.

IAGO

Cassio, drink this much more wine. I go!

He puts some coins on the table.

IAGO

What thou art planning to do with this young
girl, I chose to go home and do to my wife.
If I stay, I will not be able to
perform the deed. I go home half sober

Iago exits.

BIANCA

So, lover, this new promotion tell me.

CASSIO

Othello, my general, sees in me,
great potential. To that end, so that I
might grow as a soldier and a man,
he's laden me responsibility.
His new lieutenant he hath so made me.

BIANCA

Thou art deserving. So let's celebrate.

CASSIO

Bianca, that's what I am doing now.

BIANCA

No. I mean you and me.

CASSIO

Privately I
plan to do that later tonight, so drink.

BIANCA

Cassio, I refer to going out

for a special night. Us, going to the
theatre or maybe a new opera.
Seeing talented musicians play.

CASSIO

Theatre? Opera? Musicians? Please,
Bianca, what's wrong with thee? Feeling ill?

BIANCA

Cassio, I am just like thee. I have
intellect. I have sophistication.
I am a cultured lady. I sometimes
hide the real me to satisfy some of
my customers. But I like culture things.

CASSIO

Besides pearls?

BIANCA

Lots of men admit that
I'm a cultured lady. Growing up on
Larnaca, men would give me pearls for favors.
I got used to it.

CASSIO

Larnaca? Were you born in Cyprus?

BIANCA

Legend says that Aphrodite washed on
to the shores of Larnaca. I'm sorry
to admit this, but I have used that legend
many a time on a foreigner.
Or maybe it's true, women of Cyprus
we carry a special way about us.

CASSIO

I think thou hast a touch of the goddess
Aphrodite in your soul, Bianca.

She takes a swig from a bottle, drinks, then belches.

BIANCA

Of course, I do, Mikey. Thou knowest I
have men who had wanted to marry me.

CASSIO

Fat, rich, bald, old men.

BIANCA

Yes. And young ones too.
I am a gentlewoman, Cassio
waiting for a gentleman. Maybe thee?

CASSIO

I am a soldier, not a gentleman.

BIANCA

How dost thou feel about wife and marriage?

CASSIO

A good idea. When I find a woman,
fall in love. I will marry a virgin.

BIANCA

Virgin?

CASSIO

Yes, a virgin.

BIANCA

A virgin?
Do you hear yourself? A virgin! What do
you believe in? Social myths. Have you no
respect for your friend? Your obelisk,
your little white rooster? Does he deserve
better than an inexperienced, inept,
ignorant spoiled brat? Why would you put
your throbbing friend in an amateur's hands?
He loves you and performs for you.
He's to be cherished and given
every benefit you can afford.
Your pulsating glory stands tall for you...
and you want to give him over to some
ill-prepared socialite swearing, "I love you"?
Some silver-spooned elitist that looks in
the mirror when she should be looking into your
heart. Clumsy, awkward, sexually ignorant.
That short-tongued babbling gossip thou wants to
trust with your friend...your mentor...your manly pride?
A silly-faced jabber jaw with no sense
of desire or passion? A virgin!
And that's what you want, Michael Cassio?My advice...pay
your ducats to a real
professional and get a woman that
knows what she's doing and how to do you.

CASSIO

Bianca, for shame, a virgin can be
wisely taught. Thou knowest this. She can
discover the mysteries of her own
womanliness. I would be unlocking
her vault of desires, her carnal self.

BIANCA

O, why dost thou think I have customers?
Men like thee went to her vault, t'was empty.
Think'st thou, every girl is going to really
enjoy the erotic journey? I think not.
Look at me. I know thee. I know what you like.
Think back on your other encounters.
Were many willing to give of themselves to thee?
Thy eyes tell me no. A big fat nay. No.
How many, dear Michael, had to be coaxed?
How many begged, "I need time to think about it?"
You want a woman that is not afraid
of her own desires and wants to share
those desires with thee. Otherwise, you
will be in some new brothel, looking for
the satisfaction you cannot find home.
We strumpets will never be out of work.
Because there are men like thee that took a
chance on a virgin and found her sorely lacking.
These men end up fat, bald, and spending their
money on strumpets. Begging for a discount.

CASSIO

Zounds, I never thought of it in those terms.

BIANCA

Take a woman you know 'tis good in bed.
Mold her to your other desires. A woman
that looks good on your arm, knows how to love you.
Teach that woman, etiquette. One thing's a surety.
The bedroom will be your sanctuary.
Show her steps to being a lady.
Take her arm, guide her through the uncharted
waters of society. You will have

a woman two-fold better than any
high and mighty virgin thou might ever find.

She kisses him.

CASSIO

I hope I remember all that you said
in the morning for I am now so drunk.
I know the words that you speak are cause for care.
Something for me to truly think on.

BIANCA

Lover, don't worry, I will remind you.
We'll have plenty of time to work this through.

Black Out.

Scene 2

Piazza San Marco: A street in Venice. Roderigo is sitting in the street, moaning. Iago walks by, notices Rodrigo, stops, and returns.

IAGO

Old friend Roderigo, is't thee, I see?

RODERIGO

Ho, Lieutenant Iago, true 'tis me.

IAGO

(aside) Lieutenant, one word and I am undone.
I shall ignore it, concentrate on him.
I see you sit and lament, Roderigo.

RODERIGO

Ay me! 'Tis so true. A lamentable soul.

IAGO

Why such a long face? I would think thou to
be swimming in a sea of love.
Art thou not married?

RODERIGO

If it were only so.

IAGO

Did she not like the tune? Heard your tenor,

surely, she must have fallen in love with
the music in her ear.

RODERIGO

Would it were so.

IAGO

Maybe we should find another song.
One with a symphonic melody.
Add a choir, I'm sure she will have you.

RODERIGO

It is her father. He guards the door like
a basilisk in heat. Coiled, ready to strike.

IAGO

She never heard you sing?

RODERIGO

Nay, not a note.

IAGO

I am appalled. Such braves notes were silenced
by paternal angst. Perk up, man, the game
is not over. Surely, there is a way
to get past this fierce, green-eyed dragon.

RODERIGO

How? Oh how, Iago? Enlighten me, please.
You are older, wiser. Married. I will
gladly give you coin of my half-filled purse...
if you but teach me access. How might I
climb her garden wall and so sing in the
moonlight to her balcony window.

IAGO

How much? Good Roderigo, how much do
you value this true love? For I tell thee
'tis a surety, I have your answer,
if thou art willing to pay for privilege.

Roderigo reaches into his purse and hands Iago a coin.

RODERIGO

Here, this seems fair.

IAGO

If you seek a milkmaid.
Did not you tell me she is a lady?

RODERIGO

Yes. She is a lady.

Roderigo hands Iago more coins.

IAGO

Is that so, friend?
A lady that you like or is it love?

Iago motions with his hands for more coins. Roderigo give more coins.

IAGO

Is this a little love or a big love?
A love or infatuation or do
you want this courtship in your heart of hearts
to end for thee on the marital altar?

RODERIGO

Marriage, of course.

IAGO

Then give me more ducats.

Roderigo counts out more coins, then decides to give Iago his whole purse.

IAGO

Right, that's a bright lad. This shows me you love
her with a strong Herculean passion.
Let us examine the situation.
Her father blocks your cock. Yet she has eyes for you.

RODERIGO

She is mad about me. I just must prove
my love to her, I know she will be mine.

IAGO

She cannot but give in to a face such as yours.
Roderigo, take your heart off your sleeve.
First thing you do is win her father's love.
Trust me. Gain the father, you gain the child.
What's his weakness? What chink in his armor
can we find? Is it the lack money?

RODERIGO

No, he is prosperous.

IAGO

Social standing?

RODERIGO

He is friends with the Duke?

IAGO

Oh, this walnut
be a tough shell to split. Is't literate?

RODERIGO

He likes stories. Some soldier visits and
dines with them, tells the family war stories.

IAGO

Ah, we have found it.

RODERIGO

What have we now found?

IAGO

Books, rare books. Books of adventure, daring
do, and fantastical deeds or legends.
Bring him a book, nay two books. One for her
and one for him. 'Tis fair. Shows you thoughtful.

RODERIGO

Brilliant!

IAGO

Friend Roderigo, the books will
get you through the door. It will give you time.
Time to see the lady. Time to woo the father.
For you must woo the father before you
proceed to the girl. He must find you a
worthy gentleman for his family jewel.

RODERIGO

I am such a gentleman.

IAGO

Yes, you are.
So please, sir, waste not your time moping here.
There are books to be found to bring you cheer.

Roderigo gets up and exits in a hurry.

IAGO

What an imbecile? A thumb-sucking cretin.
I know not if this ruse will impress the
lady's obstinate father. It matters not.
In the short run, I have made coin, well done.
Still, I have obstacles to overcome.
Cassio is the Moor's lieutenant, and
I his ancient. He has no scars on his
face, this boot-licking fog-blathering factoid.
I think I want revenge. I think I do.
I find this life unfair. Can I become
a duplicitous false-face devil?
Can I even the score, on the inky
Moor. For it irks me no end. This sooty
charcoal scullion controls my destiny,
with no viable compensation and
rewards the foolish flap-eared Florentine.
I must think on this. Surely, there is a
way to mete out revenge. I will not rush
this race, for I plan to last the distance.
It must be done in such a way; I will take care.
I must smell sweet though the stink of villain fills the air.

Black Out.

Scene 3

Casa Di Brabantio: Desdemona and Brabantio are talking.

DESDEMONA
Will Othello dine with us tonight?

BRABANTIO
Yes.
He's such a wonderful storyteller.
Daughter, can you imagine seeing the
Anthropophagi? And living to tell
the tale.

DESDEMONA
You like him?

BRABANTIO
Yes, even I am
surprised by that statement. He is a Moor
and I actually value his friendship.
Certainly, a cut above other Moors
I have met. Othello seems civilized.
I know that deep down, he's a black heathen,
but he appears to have cultivation.

DESDEMONA
Maybe it is because he has travelled.

BRABANTIO

Most certainly he has had a vast and
adventurous life. Jason and his
Argonauts could not compare with this strong
sable warrior's life. I'll wager
Othello could have found the Golden Fleece
faster and returned sooner had he sought
to do so. What think you, Desdemona?

DESDEMONA

Father, I have never seen you impressed
with a man such as he. Do you think some
of his stories invented to entertain?

BRABANTIO

Oh, Desdemona, don't be cynical
I am sure there are gallons of truth in
those stories. I have met others who spoke
without an ounce of truth. It's easy to
recognize a lie. It is difficult
to deceive me. I know Venetians that
could not hold a candle to Othello's
worldly adventures. Had he lived earlier,
Marco Polo would have been his footman.
The man has dabbled in magic. Knows black
magic, knows when to use it, my daughter.
He weaves his mystic web with every tale.
I so look forward to these evenings.

DESDEMONA

Yes, Father, I see the delight on your
face when he humbly arrives at our door.

BRABANTIO

Some Moslem woman will be a very
happy wife, when he decides to marry.

DESDEMONA

You think soon he'll marry?

BRABANTIO

No. I pray not.
First, he must help us win this Cyprus war.
If a man can do it, I'm sure 'tis he.

DESDEMONA

He has the mind for it.

BRABANTIO

Not just the mind.
He has the strength of character and the
fortitude of a dozen men.
Methinks he can only die by his own hand.
He has been close to death a dozen times
yet he was able to avoid that demon.

DESDEMONA

May the future bless all his desires.

BRABANTIO

Good thoughts. We'll pray for this ebony knight.
Let's pray that he reaches all of his goals.

DESDEMONA

Father, I will add that prayer to mine own.

BRABANTIO
Daughter, thou art a good and decent girl.
Having him visit so often, I pray
his dark-sooty face does not repel thee?

DESDEMONA
Father, his is not the first black face I
have encountered. I remember our maid
Barbary, she woke me every morning.
A better face my eyes could not have seen.

BRABANTIO
Ah yes. I, too, Barbary remember.
A gentle heart. Soft words and strong hands too.
Now, I must leave you. To see the
Duke on this matter in Cyprus.
When Othello arrives show him respect.
So I am off and will return shortly.
Let's make sure our meal is delectable,
may his words make our hearts susceptible.

Black Out.

ACT V

Scene 1

Casa Di Brabantio: Desdemona and Othello are sitting and kissing.

OTHELLO

We shall be married in the San Marco
Basilica. I have made arrangements.

DESDEMONA

And you will become a Catholic?

OTHELLO

Amen. Desdemona, I'll change for you my life.
From single man to married man, from a
Muslim to a Christian. I am better
for it. You delight me. You have captured
my soul and I give that soul to you in
a Christian church with a Christian priest.

DESDEMONA

Othello, I am yours even now. *(They kiss.)*
My heart's subdu'd.

OTHELLO

I will have my ancient,
Iago sent to you for conveyance to
the cathedral. There, we shall meet and wed.
What of your father, how shall we distract him?

DESDEMONA

I'll have him run an errand. It should give
us time to prepare. A small deception
for a grand prize.

OTHELLO

My soul does rejoice.
We shall keep this secret 'till we find the
time to share our news, no need to alert foes.

DESDEMONA

You know best.

OTHELLO

Here carry this handkerchief.
As a symbol of my love.

DESDEMONA

'Tis beautiful.

OTHELLO

It is magical. T'was made in Egypt.
Worms were unlike any that do breed silk.
Strawberries symbolize a heart in love.
Its red color announces the passion
of a true love found, a true love cherished.
See the milky cream color of this silk,
it matches the true lovers' purity.
Our wedding night, we will have a feast of
strawberries and cream to celebrate our
union as newlywed husband and wife.

DESDEMONA

I'll forever treasure it.

OTHELLO

I know you will.

DESDEMONA

'Tis your first gift to me.

OTHELLO

No, chuck, I gave
you my heart long before this moment, we
shall delight in each other, for this is
the first of many. We have a lifetime
of love and sharing.

DESDEMONA

I have a gift for you.

OTHELLO

A gift for me. *(She kisses him.)* Desdemona, may that
gift multiply a thousand-fold, for that
gift will change with the vows we share. They will
be kisses given not as friend to friend,
but as husband to wife. A more precious
gift could not be shared. 'Tis a gift of our
fidelity to each other and trust.

DESDEMONA

Even so. A gift that keeps on giving.
Let it be in wedded bliss our living.

She kisses him again.

Black Out.

Scene 2

Casa Di Iago: Iago enters his home.

IAGO

Wife, my house, there's no smell of osso bucco.
I need the aroma of garlic, basil,
oregano, or parmigiana. Food.
My belly is crying I need a meal
to wipe away the hungry tears.

Emilia enters.

EMILIA

I am here, husband. What news from the Moor?
The commission is't yours? Do I feed the
lieutenant tonight. Speak, tell me the news?

IAGO

Yes, if his name be Michael Cassio,
the Florentine. The Moor has made his choice.

EMILIA

Damn. Is he a worthy recipient?

IAGO

'Tis an outrageous choice. A mathematician,
all brain, no brawn. He's never tasted dirt
of field, nor smelled smoke of cannon fire.

He can't lead men. A paragon of numbers
is he. Truth, I am known far and wide as
honest, I've fought in field with a squadron.

EMILIA

T'will tell you truly I don't understand
the Moor. 'Tis a repulsive puzzlement.
You're the victim of unkind politics.
It makes no sense; you are the better man.
Shouldn't take this lying down, rise, fight back.

IAGO

The decision has been made. There is no
turning back. He will not take away the
commission. Zounds! His word has been given.
He's a man of his word. We wait for Cassio to fall.

EMILIA

Can you mete out revenge on Cassio?

IAGO

He's innocent. Not a fault, he has no
talent as a soldier. The fault lies with
the Moor. If I were to seek revenge, it
would not be against Cassio, dear wife.
But, Emilia, I'm not a vengeful man.
I serve my country and I serve the Moor.
Now he is all eyes, no sight. Someday, he
will open those eyes and see my value.

EMILIA

Thou art honest and forthright. I love thee.
You make me proud, Iago, to be thy wife.
Lesser men would begrudge Cassio and
fall under the yoke of wicked revenge.

IAGO

You just gave me the greatest gift a wifecan give her husband.
You believe in me.
But I long for a second gift, dinner.
I want you to serve me, my appetite
cries out for a meal, cooked by your sweet hands.

Othello enters.

OTHELLO

What ho! I say is anyone at home?

IAGO

Othello, good morrow, my general.
My wife and I were talking about thee.

OTHELLO

Friend Iago. I hope kindly were your words.

IAGO

As I am honest, so they were, kind sir.
Emilia and I were discussing the
value of your presence in our Venice.
Thou art a leader of immense talent.

EMILIA

May I get you a cup of tea? Please, why
not sit and make yourself comfortable.

OTHELLO

I thank you…yes, a drink for these parched lips.

Emilia exits.

IAGO

And for mine. Sometimes, wives seem to forget.
What brings my general to my humble home?
Another commission in the offing?

OTHELLO

No. I have a request. 'Tis personal,
if you refuse, it is a surety
I will understand.

IAGO

Please, my General,
any request I will be at your service.
I am for you. What can humble Iago
do for this his Sepia General?

OTHELLO

First, good news, I join thee as a Catholic.

Emilia re-enters with a drink. A mug of tea. She hands the drink to Othello

EMILIA

Impossible. Is't true?

OTHELLO

O, yes, it's true.
I happily converted from Islam.

IAGO

So you are now a true Venetian?

OTHELLO

Iago, I am in love.

EMILIA

Impossible.
O, too much good news in so little time.

IAGO

That is wonderful news. She is Catholic?

OTHELLO

And the loveliest rose in the garden.
Her eyes sparkle when she laughs. When she speaks,
her voice sings truly like a nightingale.
It's a wonder, she loves this old black ram.

EMILIA

Congratulations. (aside) T'was a long time coming.

IAGO

Tis good news, Commander. Who's this lucky lass?
How can I be of service to you, sir?

OTHELLO

She's Senator Brabantio's daughter.
The lovely Desdemona. We would be
married tomorrow night. I ask your service.
'Tis a secret and must stay a secret,
'till after our nuptials are consummated.
I would ask you to escort my future
wife to San Marco's Basilica.
There to be wed. Can'st thou service my wish?

IAGO

Proud Othello, I am happy to aid
and abet you in your secret nuptials.
I feel like cupid aiming his arrows
at two hearts filled with loving destiny.

Let me offer my wife Emilia as
your future love's lady in waiting.

EMILIA

'Tis not necessary. I am sure the
lady has her own maid that she prefers.

OTHELLO

I would not want to impose on thy wife.

IAGO

Tut! 'Tis no imposition. There are things
these women do on their wedding day that
needs the hand of a woman who has walked
the bridle path. Is it not so, Emilia?

EMILIA

Kind Othello, I am happy to help.
Let us be of service to your new love.

OTHELLO

'Tis thoughtful, but I just need an escort.

IAGO

It will be your wedding night. Who knows what
things women want in their preparation?
Please, sir, let my wife help your future wife?
O, as a husband, I will tell thee true,
we can never have too much help in
satisfying the needs of a woman.

OTHELLO

True. 'Tis done. Well said. I thank you, Iago.
Now, friend, there's errands you must accomplish.

IAGO
Ink and paper that I miss not a jot.

Iago exits.

EMILIA
You would marry this child Desdemona?

OTHELLO
Are you not happy for me, Emilia?

EMILIA
What is to become of us?

OTHELLO
We are finished. As I had informed you.

EMILIA
I will tell her of us. I will tell her
of how we cuckold my loving husband.
All the nasty, dirty, little things we
did together, I will share with your bride
and we will see how eager she is to
marry the Moor. You will always be mine.

Othello grabs her by the throat. He chokes her.

OTHELLO
On pain of death, you should censure your thoughts.
If you but breathe one syllable to my
bride, I will make your death miserable.
Understood?

She nods.

OTHELLO

I have but to sense an inkling of your
betrayal and I will be revenged, is't clear?

She nods. Othello lets her go; she recovers from her choking.

OTHELLO

Ahhhh, Emilia, you are so sensitive
to my feelings. It pleases me that you
want nothing for me but my happiness.

Iago returns with ink and paper.

IAGO

Ink and paper. Let us confer on the
necessities of your new marriage, sir.
So tell me, what errands, must I complete?
Her escort I'll be for Othello's pride
Desdemona will be the perfect bride.

Black Out.

Scene 3

Palazzo Ducale: The Duke's Palace. Cassio enters.

CASSIO

Your Grace called for me.

DUKE

Yes, young Cassio?
Are you not Othello's new lieutenant?

CASSIO

Yes, sir. I'm newly commissioned, my Lord.

DUKE

We here congratulate you, Michael Cassio.
There is mischief afoot, we need the Moor.
We have sent messengers to his house to
no avail. Time is of the essence.

CASSIO

How may I help, Your Lordship?

DUKE

Turks. It's Othello.
We must find Othello! Turks, make for Cyprus.

CASSIO

I see, the valiant general doesn't know this?
So the counsel and the Duke, must have him?

DUKE

The Moor knows the fortitude of the place.
We have a substitute there, yet we feel,
more capable hands are held by Othello,
his embrace of the situation will
hopefully nullify any attempts
to eradicate our post with Ottomans.

CASSIO

Grave news indeed. How may I assist thee?

DUKE

Find Othello, it's imperative. Now!
Go to his haunts, ferret him out, and bring
him hither. We wish to discuss with him
what preparations should be made so to
ensure that land gained doesn't become land lost.

CASSIO

Yes, sir.

DUKE

Friend Cassio, as quickly as
possible. If he is in the lap of
a strumpet, pull him away. If he be
drinking the last dregs of the finest wine
in Venice, pull him away. If he be
at the theatre or opera, listening
to the finest music played by the
finest musicians, so pull him away.

Bring him here as quickly as possible
for this is of the most dire and the
most immediate of consequences.

CASSIO
No matter where he be, I will him find.
though his humor be surly or unkind.

Black Out.

Scene 4

Casa Di Brabantio: Emilia is brushing Desdemona's hair.

EMILIA

So you enchanted the ebony knight.

DESDEMONA

Lucky.

EMILIA

Methinks you know your strengths and allure.

DESDEMONA

I feel so lucky to have God bless me.
This magnificent man sees something in
me that pleases him.

EMILIA

He's one of a kind.
There are Moors here in Venice, but I dare
say none can compare to your Othello.
A man of experience. Like a wild
untamed beast when his ire has been set on,
yet a domesticated kitten when
he is at peace. He'll make a fine husband.

DESDEMONA

Of late, his life has been so erratic.
I hope that I might bring calm to his soul.
Once we are married, I look forward to
us building a family. I would love
a houseful of little Othellos that
play and run and jump around our home.

EMILIA

Truly a sight to see. Tonight, we bring
you across the threshold of single life
into the sorority of married
women. I pray you listen to your man
and fill his needs. An empty cup may
cause a man to seek a thirst quencher in
other taverns and in other cups.

DESDEMONA

Somehow, I think that Othello and I,
we will not have that problem. I am his,
body and soul. I feel it is ordained
by the heavens.

EMILIA

Then, m'lady, you're blessed.

DESDEMONA

Emilia, recover please my veil.

Emilia exits.

DESDEMONA

Why should I live a life of normalcy?
Why should I be a normal Venetian?
Hemmed in by social architecture,

have I a chance for a great adventure?
Have I a chance to be a hero's wife?
Fortune smiles, so I change my dull future,
and marry this sepia sentinel.
Care I if white men look on in disgust,
Anger, and envy? Not a whit, not a whit.
Care I if Italians call this union
Monstrous? Not a jot, certain not a jot.
Step away from this safe pedestrian
Calm, boring life, into a new world.
My heart's a pioneer for love. O, yes.
An explorer in uncharted waters
Of destiny. I beheld Adonis
And my soul soared. Strong emotions climbed
like Icarus to the sun, with the soft
simplicity of a kiss. Soft brown lips.
I felt the woolly mammoth, seize, expand
my exhilaration of womanhood.
Yes, I will wrap my legs around his waist
and let his manly thrusts consummate me
into wifely pleasures. Exultations
of ecstasy. Othello's life surely
will lift my circumstance from the mundane.
His heart has been touched, I, like a candle,
has he lit. This light which illumes all my
darkness. No, I flicker not, but am a
beacon of what is yet to come, unseen
I touched his heart and know primal instinct
of Eve, discovering Adam. Feeling
as God's first woman's soul must unite with
first man's soul. My very existence will
push boundaries of what this world thinks it
knows, believes, and can endure. Tonight, we
must cross the threshold of the commonplace,
we rise, so to meet extraordinary.

Tonight, I become my own hero.
Open I, my true self, to a man, who
will redefine boundaries of true love.
Tonight, this little white virgin marries
the big black warrior knowing that some
white Christian men will see and will hate me,
black Muslim women burden with anger.
My father will think I am bewitched,
I suppose I am. Yes. O, yes, I am.
Bewitched, in possibilities of such
infinite desires, now satisfied.
I will hold my head high, unafraid to
embrace. Unafraid to challenge the world
for the sake of our love and our true hearts.
O, my God, Yes! I'm a lucky woman.
Tonight, I go a girl and end as wife,
I meet my husband and start a new life.

Lights Fade.

In another part of the house, Roderigo enters singing, playing the mandolin, with a book bag over his shoulder.

RODERIGO *(sings)*
Brabantio! 'Tis I.
Under the greenwood tree
Who loves to lie with me,
And turn his merry note
Unto the sweet birds' throat
Come hither, Modulate…
Come hither, come hither!
Here shall she see no enemy
But lover and us together.

Iago enters, Roderigo stops singing.

IAGO

Roderigo? What are you doing here?

RODERIGO

Come to gift my future father-in-law
what most he should have, song and new rare books.
But I am asking you that same question.
What do you want here? Are you in love with
the fair Desdemona too? You have known
of my suit, now you usurp my title.

IAGO

Nincompoop! Remember not I am wed?

RODERIGO

Then tell me, false Iago, why are you here?

IAGO

The lady you spoke of, the lady that you
so wanted, sir, is Desdemona?

RODERIGO

Yes. You know 'tis true. So why are you here?

IAGO

God bless all the saints! I am here for you.

RODERIGO

For me?

IAGO

To intercede and soften her
father's heart, so that you might win her love.

RODERIGO

You'd do that for me?

IAGO

And not ask for one
ducat in return. I will tell you this.
Othello, the Moor, wants to marry her.

RODERIGO

Black soldier I saw coming here to dine?

IAGO

You ne'er told me the soldier was a Moor.
I could have helped sooner had I known.

RODERIGO

I didn't say it, but t'was thinking it.

IAGO

O, tis no matter now. I forsooth have
spoken on your behalf. I hate the Moor.
I should not want to see that Barbary
horse defile such a virginal and sweet,
lily-white flower as Desdemona.
She belongs in the arms of thee, not some
grubby, sooty, black charcoal foreigner.

RODERIGO

Of me? Thou art truly for me, Iago.

IAGO

You are the more worthy man. Do I lie?

RODERIGO

No. Thou speaks true. I am such a hero.

IAGO

Of course, you are, strong, intelligent, rich.
Only you can satisfy the needs of
such a sweet, lovely, and youthful spirit.

RODERIGO

'Tis so true. I love her for her fine foot,
straight leg, and the purity of her soul.

IAGO

O, trust me, my friend, as an honest man,
I will intercede for you, open the
senator's eyes and make a clear path to
his daughter's chambers, that you may be her
husband. Not this ink-black interloper.

RODERIGO

'Tis good, 'tis very good. You'd do this for me?

IAGO

Without payment. We Venetians must be
bound to each other or these immigrants
will wash to our shores and take our women.
They are not gifts for others to have, no.
We must be diligent and vigilant.

EMILIA *(off stage)*

Iago, I need you, please come here.

IAGO

Go now…leave me to my plan. Her father
is not here now. On his return, I will
sue for thee the chance to woo his lovely
daughter. Then let thy natural charms take
effect. I am sure she will be all yours.

RODERIGO
I go. But I will return tomorrow.

IAGO
'Tis all the time I need. 'Till tomorrow.

Roderigo exits.

IAGO
Tomorrow will be too late. Sad but true.

Emilia enters.

EMILIA
Iago, we are ready, and we need you.
We must now to church, for the bride is due.

Black Out.

Scene 5

Casa Di Cassio: Cassio enters. Bianca is in his bed.

CASSIO
I forgot you were here. You must now go.

BIANCA
Love, you have an urgent air about you.

CASSIO
I have been given a task by the Duke.
I must succeed. I can waste no time on thee.

BIANCA
Can I help you in this task?

CASSIO
I think not.
I'm on a mission, I must find Othello.

BIANCA
What is the hurry?

Cassio finds his sword.

CASSIO
I come from the Duke!
We may, Cyprus, return. Turmoil exists.

BIANCA

But why must you return with Othello?
Can he not use other men in your place?

CASSIO

I am his lieutenant.

BIANCA

But what of us?

CASSIO

Bianca, I am a soldier, sweet heart.

BIANCA

Will you not marry me before you leave?

CASSIO

Woman, I am talking of war and you
are talking of bouquets and a wedding.

He fumbles with his scabbard. Bianca helps him.

BIANCA

Michael Cassio, you forget I am
from Cyprus. I grew up in war. There is
always time for a wedding. I know you
love me and you know it to be true too.

CASSIO

I know no such thing. I know I am a
soldier and I am newly appointed
officer. I don't think my general
will take kindly to me announcing I
want to marry you.

BIANCA

Michael, you need a woman in your life.
I am that woman. Trust me, my soldier.

CASSIO

Bianca, 'tis not the time to debate
my future. I am on a mission, it
is critical I find Othello and
deliver him to our Lord, the Duke.

BIANCA

So, Mikey, shall I wait for your return?
I can relieve any anxiety
you might have before you leave for this war.

CASSIO

No, woman. I want thee gone when I return.
I have no time for your womanly ways.

BIANCA

Before you go, a remembrance.

He goes to her and she kisses him. It is a passionate kiss. Cassio exits.

BIANCA

T'was not the kiss of a disinterested
soldier. He has his plans, and I have mine.
I know men better than I know the streets
of Venice. I will return to my home
in Cyprus, and I will lay a plan that
includes one Michael Cassio, husband.
Why, men are really such simple creatures.
All a woman need know is where to touch
when to touch and how to touch, then, he will

give what must be given. I know the isle
of Cyprus. I'll make my way to a ship,
sail home, and in my own city, I will
use it to my advantage. No one knows
Cyprus better than I. And no one knows
where its treasures lie. I will wake up his
senses under the Cyprus moon and take
this bachelor to wedding bliss.
I move closer to my goal with every kiss.

Scene 6

Basilica San Marco: Othello enters alone. He is dressed in white and wears a turban.

OTHELLO

I have been in the company of many
beautiful woman and always found them
lacking till now. A beautiful face asks
no demands and expects preference,
but not this girl. She has the common touch
with an elegant hand. She does not act
like a pampered, rich, coddled, selfish girl.
My ebony face does not repel her.
The hue of my skin invites her to me.
'Tis true she loves me. True.
A righteous love I feel so worthy of.
I had dreamt if I put aside old
ways of my past, turned over a new leaf,
that Allah might reward me. Here she is,
Desdemona is my timely reward.

Lights up on Desdemona in the church. She takes off her cape to reveal her wedding dress.

OTHELLO

I do repent women I took in war,
the wives I used in peace and the girls I
brought to womanhood. 'Tis time for a new

Othello. A man that looks back from the
mirror and smiles at what he sees.
I am capable of being that man.
I am that man because of this woman.
This lady will be my wife. I thank God
for my revelation. So I now set
aside the name of Allah. I will use
the Christian name of God. For they are one
and the same. For what's really in a name?

The lights change.

Othello crosses to Desdemona in church.

OTHELLO
So, my love, we embark on our nuptials.

DESDEMONA
Dost thou feel it is unlucky to see
your bride just before the ceremony?

OTHELLO
Superstitious, I am not, my lovely.

DESDEMONA
You are pleased with me?

OTHELLO
Yes, of course, I am.

DESDEMONA
And you are pleased with your new religion?

OTHELLO
'Tis for you loveliest of the lovelies.

DESDEMONA

Then let me discard the last vestiges
of your past. May I remove your turban?

OTHELLO

Only if it pleases you.

She unwraps his turban.

DESDEMONA

You please me.
As we join hands and hearts, we join our souls.
So we will venture as wife and husband,
to a world of our own making. Let us
strip away artifice, see each as one.

OTHELLO

What is it about thee that makes it us?
I think maybe 'tis the truth in thine eyes
or could it be the knowledge from your smile,
like a primrose, fragrant yet subtle, O
you carry me to myself. I knowing
the elegance and beauty of your heart
captivate me and encircle my hope.
Riveting my will to the source of its
fountain. The golden hair tosses of thy
head invite me wonderful adventures.
We will unite under the eye of God,
knowing that it has been preordained.

Desdemona wipes Othello's brow with the handkerchief he gave her.

DESDEMONA

Blessed by the certainty of this union
we move as one. Today I celebrate

our beginnings. Acknowledge the very
first moment you breathed life into my heart.
So open your eyes and say yes to the
start of our journey. I knew we had to be.
I just did not know how. I thank you for
all the minutes we shared and look to the
future for all our years. You're my soul's cause.

Othello and Desdemona cross to the church altar. The lights change.
They stand before the priest. Emilia is standing in the church as a witness. On
the other side of the stage stands Iago. Iago turns downstage. The lights change.

IAGO
It's thus my fate that God has intervened
to give me my revenge. The sable Moor
loves this girl as does the beetle-headed
Roderigo, the same girl, love. The same girl!
O, Jove laughs at this. I could not ask for
better circumstances. How can I use
this to my advantage? So must I now
gain the trust of the Moor to use him for
my own devices. He entrusted me
the delivery of his fiancée
to this church. 'Tis a brick I will build on.
Roderigo thinks I know how to guide
her heart. There is profit in this. I will
claim his purse for my own. So I will see
that he puts money in my purse.
O, I can see the future, it looks bleak
for this thick-lipped and wooly-headed Moor.
I will use him; I will use him for my
own sport. I must calm myself, for 'tis too
perfect to be true. I must go into
this with a clear head and a sound mind.
Patience is the key. Let this fish bite and

swallow the hook. A hook in the belly
is far better than a hook in the lip.
For surely a strong fish can yank the hook
from his mouth and survive with but a scar
of the encounter. But let that fish swallow
the hook, he will rip apart his insides ere
he gets away, I want to see his
incarnadine insides laid bare on my table.
I will fillet this fish ere I eat the meal.
He's mine, it starts tonight. This holy night.
The night of his wedding. I am resolved.
For the future of my life has been solved.

The priest blesses Desdemona's ring, He puts the ring on an open Bible he is holding. Othello takes the ring from the Bible and places it on Desdemona's finger.

The lights change as Othello kisses Desdemona.

Lights go to black on the priest.

Lights go to black on Emilia.

Lights fade on the Iago.

A spotlight holds on Desdemona and Othello, as their marriage kiss lingers.

Black Out.

END OF PLAY

THE TEARS

of

SHYLOCK

Dedicated to

Immigrants seeking freedom
and a shared humanity.

Thanks to

Ben Donenberg
Don Geisinger
Karen Harris
E. Jack Kaplan
Rabbi Steven Carr Reuben

The Tears of Shylock was performed as a reading at the Matrix Theatre on April 9, 2019, with the following cast:

JESSICA	Sophia Wackerman
LORENZO	Michael Proctor
SHYLOCK	Bruce Cervi
OLD GOBBO	Erick Kilpatrick
GUINEVERE	Angela K. Thomas
OTHELLO	Thomas Anthony Jones
RODERIGO LOPEZ	Stephen Spiegel
NARRATOR	Ron Brewington

The Tears of Shylock was performed as a Zoom Reading and recorded on July 15, 2020, with the following cast and is available to view on YouTube.

JESSICA	Jessica Moreno
LORENZO	Michael Proctor
SHYLOCK	Bruce Cervi
OLD GOBBO	Ted Lange
GUINEVERE	Keena Ferguson
OTHELLO	Thomas Anthony Jones
RODERIGO LOPEZ	Stephen Spiegel
NARRATOR	Mary Lange

AUTHOR'S NOTES

How can a nation of immigrants lock up other immigrants who are in a search of a better life in our country? How can we put brown children in de facto concentration camps and separate them from their parents who are seeking our American dream? This present-day inhumanity is actually a reflection of the universal plight immigrants have suffered for all ages. My quest was how to best address the immutability of this injustice and present it to theatre audiences.

History offers many opportunities to reveal the story of immigrants seeking asylum. I obviously could have written a play regarding what is happening today, but I felt that this was too specific and I wanted to examine the universality of immigrants. In 1619, Africans coming to America did not come freely; they were kidnapped and relegated into slavery. As I pondered my choices, it became obvious that the Jewish immigrant was truly the global immigrant, having been immigrants in just about every country in the world.

My love of all things Shakespeare steered me toward Shylock, and *The Merchant of Venice*, considered one of Western literature's most vilified immigrants in Venice, Italy. As I began my research, the parallels between the treatment of immigrants in the 1500s with what is happening today was eerily synonymous. The word *ghetto* comes from the Italian word *iron works* and has evolved to denote where the lowest ethnic race in a country live. Jews in Venice were locked behind iron gates at 6 p.m. and not released until the morning. Jews were not allowed to drink at the water fountain in the center of the city. Jews were restricted to professions deemed appropriate for their stature regardless of their talents or aspirations.

Once I discovered these similarities, Shylock became my vessel to examine and reveal the mindset of the immigrant through my play, *The Tears of Shylock*. I present Shylock's point of view on all the negative anti-Semitic words that Shakespeare wrote about Jews. *The Merchant of Venice* in the 1500s England was considered a comedy, and Shakespeare's racial slurs were a source of ridicule and laughter for the elite of England. Shylock's fate at the end of the play to become a Christian or die exemplifies sixteenth-century Christian superiority and humor.

I also wanted to explore the mindset of the children of immigrants. To that end, I contrasted the relationship of Shylock and Jessica with Shylock's servant, Old Gobbo and his daughter, Guinevere. Old Gobbo had a son named Lancelot, so following the King Arthur legend, I invented Guinevere. Children of immigrants find themselves in a unique position of wishing to assimilate into a new culture while being taught to honor and respect their own culture. In my research, I came across a real-life Jewish doctor who lived in England, Roderigo Lopez. Lopez represents how immigrants find ways to survive and conform into a new culture but retain their ethnicity.

The Tears of Shylock explores the agelessness of prejudice and racism embedded in our country. The discrimination of the past is the discrimination of the present, and my hope is to bring awareness to these issues and start a journey that will transform our country to a new level of shared humanity and empathy.

SYNOPSIS

Immigrants are required to be locked behind gates at curfew. They are scorned by the mainstream culture. They are only allowed certain professions and are required to wear red hats. The plight of immigrants in Trump's 2020 is not that far removed from the Jews in Venice in 1594. *The Tears of Shylock* is my back story of Shakespeare's *The Merchant of Venice* from the point of view of Shylock.

DRAMATIS PERSONAE

Jessica is Shylock's daughter.
Lorenzo is Jessica's lover.
Shylock is a money lender.
Old Gobbo is Shylock's servant.
Guinevere is Old Gobbo's daughter.
Othello is a black Moorish general.
Roderigo Lopez is a Marrano posing as a doctor.

ACT I

Scene 1

The scene opens in the dark with the sound of a woman's voice praying in Aramaic, the Kol Nidrei. It is the voice of JESSICA, Shylock's daughter. As she speaks, a light slowly come up on her.

JESSICA

Kol Nidrei:
Ve'esarei, Ush'vuei, Vacharamei, Vekonamei, Vekinusei, Vechinuyei.
D'indarna, Ud'ishtabana, Ud'acharimna, Ud'assarna Al nafshatana

On the other side of the stage, a male voice recites the Lord's Prayer. This is LORENZO; as he speaks, a light slowly comes up on him.

LORENZO

Lord's Prayer:
Our father who art in heaven, hallowed be thy name.
Thy kingdom come,
thy will be done, on earth as it is in heaven.

She stands and moves toward center stage.

JESSICA

Miyom Kippurim zeh, ad Yom Kippurim haba aleinu letovah
Bechulhon Icharatna vehon, Kulhon yehon sharan

He stands and moves toward center stage.

LORENZO
Give us this day our daily bread and forgive us our trespasses as we forgive them that trespass against us.

JESSICA
Sh'vikin sh'vitin, betelin umevutalin, lo sheririn v'lo kayamin

LORENZO
Lead us not into temptation but deliver us from evil. For thine is the kingdom, the power and the glory forever and ever. Amen.

JESSICA
Nidrana lo nidrei, V'essarana lo essarei
Ush'vuatana lo shevuot.

Jessica is now standing in front of Lorenzo. There is darkness all around them except for the light that shines on them. They kiss. During the kiss, the lights change; it is daytime. She breaks the kiss, and they look into each other's eyes.

LORENZO
It started with a kiss.

JESSICA
Did it, my love?

LORENZO
My soul opened like soft petals blooming
from a fragrant thorn-less blushing virgin rose.
Did not our lips touching inspire thee?

JESSICA
Nay…I protest. I was yours ere that perfect
moment arrived.

LORENZO

Is't true? Tell me how is that possible?

JESSICA

O, search thy memory…t'was the first time,
Your eyes fell on me.

LORENZO

At the well of the San Marco Piazza?

JESSICA

I first saw thee drinking cool spring water
from that well…and like Eve's forbidden fruit,
the forbidden waters that sprung from that
well, prohibited to all Jews, would I
test caution? For being a proud Jewess,
I would risk sipping water from thy ladle.
In that instance, so far from my ghetto,
lost in the magic of thy Christian eyes,
I would cast aside all that I knew then
to be with you. But being taboo from
the dark Hebrew tribe, I could only wish
to be Lorenzo's solitary flower in
thy private and cherished secret garden.

LORENZO

From fairest creatures my desire increase
That there by beauty's rose might never die.
I take you in my empty waiting arms
to fill your mouth with passion's loving charms.

He kisses her.

JESSICA

So, Lorenzo' do you really love me?

LORENZO

Si, of course, 'tis one hundred percent true.

JESSICA

How?

LORENZO

How?

JESSICA

Yes, how? I ask thee once again?

LORENZO

How do I love thee? Let me...

JESSICA

Count the ways!

LORENZO

I love thee to

JESSICA

the depth

LORENZO

and

JESSICA

breadth

LORENZO

and

JESSICA

height,

LORENZO

My soul can reach.

JESSICA

When feeling?

LORENZO

Out of sight.
For the ends...

JESSICA

and being and...

LORENZO

Ideal grace.
I...

JESSICA

Love thee?

LORENZO

To the level of

JESSICA

Every day's most quiet need

LORENZO

By sun

JESSICA

and candlelight...

LORENZO

I love thee...

JESSICA

Freely?

LORENZO

As men strive for right. I love thee

JESSICA

Purely…

LORENZO

As they turn from praise.

JESSICA

I love thee

LORENZO

With the passion

JESSICA

Put to use in my old griefs

LORENZO

And with my childhood's faith,

JESSICA/ LORENZO

I love thee (both laugh)

LORENZO

With a love, I seem to lose
With my lost saints.

JESSICA

I love thee with the breadth
smiles, tears of my life! O, Prince of codpieces.

LORENZO

And if God choose, I shall but love thee
Better after death.

They kiss.

LORENZO

My God is a merciful God, he gave
me you, I want to share his tenets like
morning dew. O, Jessica, come away.
Let us leave Venice. Share my Christian God.

JESSICA

Lorenzo, thou asks for the Oak, I am
but an acorn. My father has rooted
me here in Ghetto Novo as his prize.

LORENZO

Give me like the cool rain that showers and
feeds the desert, I promise thou will ably find
an oasis in my Lord Jesus Christ.

JESSICA

I'm Levantine, Lorenzo. Thy eyes shine,
the timbre of thy thoughts, the essence of
thy every heart beat engulfs my naked passion.
But you ask too much. Should I step away
from a thousand years of a Jew's heritage?
O, change thy thought, sweet Lorenzo, that I
may change not my religion, yet love thee.

LORENZO

If thou bring Jesus into thy bosom,
Will not thou see the glory of what I know?
I think so. Lovely Jessica...convert.

JESSICA

I will consider, if you take a step.

LORENZO

A step?

JESSICA

One simple step for thy true love.

LORENZO

I stand with elephant ears; I listen to satisfy.

JESSICA

Give up the swine.

LORENZO

All of it?

JESSICA

Yes.

LORENZO

Bacon too?

JESSICA

Including the oink. Change what you now eat.
I would cook kosher in our house, my love.
Kosher blesses thy mind and thy body.
Fortifies the spirit and thy soul, love.
O, give up thy affinity for pork.
Let not one morsel pass those lips I love
to kiss. Let me give all myself to thee
and to that Jew Jesus. He fed with fish,
not with swine, and the multitude ate well.

Do this for me, and I will consider
ending my life as a Jewess. So will
I leave the synagogue for thy cathedral.

LORENZO
No pork chops, no ribs, no pork loin. All gone?

She nods and smiles.

JESSICA
Gone like the wind.

LORENZO
Jessica, thee ask too much. I love ham.

JESSICA
Is not Lorenzo, asking me to walk
away from my father, my tribe, my life
for Christianity, asking too much?

LORENZO
But I know the benefits of my religion.

JESSICA
Love asks for compromise and untarnished trust,
Let its flower bloom and turn not to dust.

Black Out.

Scene 2

SHYLOCK is at a table counting his money and making notations in a ledger. OLD GOBBO enters.

OLD GOBBO

Master Shylock, I bring thee a message
from Senor Bassanio. 'Tis urgent.

SHYLOCK

Of course, it's urgent. Christians want me to
jump at their beck and call.

Old Gobbo hands Shylock a letter, Shylock reads.

OLD GOBBO

Good news, my lord?

SHYLOCK

He wants to make a loan. O, these Christians,
quick to take a Jew's money and slow to
repay the debt.

OLD GOBBO

Bassanio seems to be a good man. Is he not trustworthy?

SHYLOCK

He is a Christian. Goodness only goes
So far, ere their natural tendencies

to distrust a Jew over takes their heart.
Prejudices enflame their reason and
common sense is undone by emotion.
Still I must admit…I like them being
in my debt. Therefore, would I could charge higher
interest to widen my lovely profit.

OLD GOBBO

I have seen this Christian Bassanio
about the Rialto. He seems to be
a good, fair man. An honest, forthright man.

SHYLOCK

Listen to me, you offspring of Hagar,
we must always with a jaundiced eye look
at Christians, for they will use a sweet tongue
a soft eye to lure you into their trap.
They are a boil, a plague on the hind parts
of a rank hog. A pale-faced carbuncle.
First chance they get to draw and quarter thee,
they will subvert the law to gain their ends
and precipitate thy final demise.

OLD GOBBO

Yes, Master Shylock.

SHYLOCK

If I lend this man
Bassanio ducats, I must make sure
his collateral is worthy. A man
must give up what he values most and that
ensures the debt be paid. Remember this
Old Gobbo, you and I are immigrants
here in Cannaregio. The gates to
this ghetto are locked at six o'clock.

The good news is it keeps the gentiles out.
The other news, we are like animals
in a cage. Never forget, Old Gobbo.

OLD GOBBO
Yes, m'lord. Shall I tell his messenger
you will meet? Or shall I send him away?

SHYLOCK
Yes. We can meet. I will see this debtor,
My hungry Christian friend, we'll discover
his need for ducats is pathetical
Now, what to ask for my collateral?

Old Gobbo exits. Shylock goes back to his ledger.

Black Out.

Scene 3

Jessica is laying a boy's outfit on a chair.

JESSICA
What, Guinevere! What ho, Guinevere!

Guinevere enters.

GUINEVERE
Does my mistress call my name?

JESSICA
Soundly too.
Please help me dress for the masque.

GUINEVERE
Did I not hear thy father advice thee
against this festival?

JESSICA
Tut, tut, my dear.
Since when does a daughter heed every word,
spewed from a father's throat. He endeavors
to imprison all my best parts with a
Chasity belt, and I will have none of it.

GUINEVERE
Mistress, these are boys' clothes. I feel deception.

JESSICA

I must use this festival to hide my
true heart. I cover my face with a mask,
and I go in secret to meet a friend.
The night has a thousand eyes, but daylight
shines on the shadows. Deception is my tool.

Guinevere dresses Jessica as a young boy.

GUINEVERE

For Christian Lorenzo? Not Lorenzo!

JESSICA

Yes, how did you know? What gave me away?
I hope my father knows not, or I am undone.

GUINEVERE

No, mistress, I think thy father knows not.
I saw Lorenzo loitering about
our door with two men. I believe to be
young Gratiano and Salerio,
and there I saw the eyes of Lorenzo
casts love longing looks to your balcony.

JESSICA

I have ventured beyond the bounds of love.
now must I look to convert and marry.

GUINEVERE

O, mistress, I cannot help thee in this
dark charade. It will anger thy father
and go hard on me. He will know I was
your accomplice. Your secret confidant.

JESSICA

No such thing will he know, I assure you.

GUINEVERE

O, I will be beaten, if he finds out.
Have you not seen the yellow man here about?

JESSICA

What yellow man? Pray tell a yellow man?

GUINEVERE

O, he is a merchant here in Venice.
Mister Yee trading a month in our ghetto.

JESSICA

Why speak you of a yellow man to me?

GUINEVERE

Mister Yee sells or trades jade, Chinese herbs
and speaks most eloquently of life.
Mister Yee is a Buddhist philosopher.

JESSICA

A Buddhist? Mister Yee?

GUINEVERE

Yes. His ancestors knew Marco Polo.
He has been talking to me of life.
He has shared his Buddhists' sayings with me.
"Three things cannot long be hidden,
the sun, the moon and the truth."

JESSICA

Hand me that box.

GUINEVERE

Which one?

JESSICA

The one my father carved.

Guinevere crosses to a table with two boxes. She picks up the wooden box and crosses back to Jessica. Jessica opens it and takes out a few ducats. She puts some coins in Guinevere's hands.

JESSICA

So do not a thing till you hear from me.
Coins for silence, steel Guinevere, your courage.
Screw that courage to the sticking place, friend.
Will thee not be a soldier for true love?

GUINEVERE

Did you steal these ducats from thy father?

JESSICA

I never steal. This is from my dowry.
A bride cannot steal from her own dowry.
No need to worry of the sun and moon.

GUINEVERE

Let truth grovel for moonlight or sunlight.
The common sense of my mind says 'tis not
a good idea. But the romance in my
heart cries out to aid and abet thee.
I see the joy in your eyes. I recognize
thy heart's desire and I will help thee.

JESSICA

I thank you, Miss G.

GUINEVERE

For three ducats more?

Jessica goes into the wooden box and gets three more coins and gives then to Guinevere.

JESSICA

'Tis done, Guinevere, for a healthy price.
Count thy coins and let all of that suffice.

Guinevere counts her money and then she finishes dressing Jessica.

Black Out.

ACT II
Scene 1

Shylock enters looking for Old Gobbo.

SHYLOCK
Old Gobbo! What ho, Gobbo!

Old Gobbo enters.

OLD GOBBO
Master Shylock?

SHYLOCK
Bring me my good wine. Now, I celebrate.

OLD GOBBO
Master, do you drink to the festival?

SHYLOCK
I drink to the demise of my enemy.

OLD GOBBO
I am glad you're in hearty spirits, for
I have sad news.

SHYLOCK
You can't disrupt my joy.
no news will break or deflate my happiness.

OLD GOBBO

I'm glad on it.

SHYLOCK

Old Gobbo, speak, please,
let's hear thy news.

OLD GOBBO

'Tis not for me to say.
My daughter is't clarion for this call.
Shall fetch her. All particulars she knows.

He exits.

SHYLOCK

Nothing can soil the bright feelings I have
for my new client. This Bassanio
has asked me for three thousand ducats.
For which he cannot on his own repay.
So he has Antonio guarantee
the bond. Antonio, my Christian foe.
He hath hindered me, disgraced me.
For what reason? His racial animus.
This enemy's passion is tedious,
He scorns my nation. In Venice, what be
immigrants? How must I survive in a
hostile city? Rancor abounds in a
country that needs you and hates that you are
the answer to its domestic problems.
A city that builds walls to lock you in,
wants to use you unaffected by guilt.
Their world on the backs of Jews has been built.
Leaders who know not how to simply add.
Gentiles confused by subtraction and at
a loss for numbers to reach reasonable sums.

Skilled by division, thriving on the art
of mendacity. I stand all alone.
Gentiles planting seeds that divide the public
craving and wanting my mental powers,
yet these cretins take no steps to educate
their minds on the craft of increasing wealth.
So I advise Christian politicians
on how to invest their gold. I counsel
gentile investors on numbers that are
a puzzle to them, clear as a road map
to me. And they all hate me for it.
This Antonio is the crystal-clear
personification of their dark hate.
So I ask for a bond. If he cannot
repay me my ducats, I may slice a
pound of his putrid flesh from his person.
Separating from his anatomy
any part I chose. Arrogance and false
superiority fill their plates as
they eat from the table of plenty.
Big fat roasted pigs they carve like cannibals
with gout, and fill their bellies with their brethren.
May I slice a pound of meat for my delight?
So we shall see. If luck holds for this gentile,
I miss my certain chance for fish bait.
But if Jehovah blesses me, I will
with a pound of flesh satisfy the bill.

Old Gobbo enters with Guinevere.

OLD GOBBO
Master, my daughter has a tale to tell.

288

GUINEVERE

Forgive me, Master Shylock, I knew not
the results as my mistress made her plans.

SHYLOCK

What plans? Where is my daughter? So tell me?

GUINEVERE

Gone, kind sir.

SHYLOCK

Where? Speak child, share thy news?

GUINEVERE

Nay. I am so afraid. Thou wilt beat me.

SHYLOCK

Nonsense. I will beat you if you don't speak.

GUINEVERE

See, Father. I told you.

SHYLOCK

Come here, my child.
Here is a ducat, you share your news.

GUINEVERE

Thy daughter has joined the night's festival.
She's put on a mask and dressed as a boy
and added her voice to their revelry.

SHYLOCK

Against my wishes? I asked her to close
windows, lock doors, and she disobeys me?

OLD GOBBO

There is more. There is more, O, there is more.

GUINEVERE

No. Father no, I can't, he will beat me.

SHYLOCK

My child, I add three ducats to your palm.

GUINEVERE

She goes to wed in secret.

SHYLOCK

Wed?

GUINEVERE

In secret.

SHYLOCK

Who?

GUINEVERE

Lorenzo of Santa Croce.

SHYLOCK

A gentile? This can't be. She will not wed.

GUINEVERE

It is a surety.

SHYLOCK

Where do they meet?

OLD GOBBO

We know not, Master Shylock.

GUINEVERE

She blended
into the crowd, like new fallen soft snow,
And so became a part of the party.
She has disappeared.

SHYLOCK

Clothes gone?

GUINEVERE

No. No, sir.
She took some ducats to sustain herself.

SHYLOCK

My money. My daughter takes my money.
Prompted no doubt by greedy Lorenzo.
Foolish girl. She is bewitched. Take these too.

Shylock hands Guinevere more coins.

SHYLOCK

You've done well by me. I must find Tubal.
What my Jessica plans is not moral.

Shylock exits out of the house. Guinevere counts her coins. Old Gobbo exits into the house.

Black Out.

Scene 2

Inside the cathedral, Jessica and Lorenzo stand and look around.

JESSICA

So this is my new church?

LORENZO

Cathedral.
San Marco Cathedral. Our cathedral.

JESSICA

Or we could
just call it a big church. A real big church.

LORENZO

Yes, we could, sweet Jessica. Yes, we could.
How do you feel? Are you ready to become a Catholic?

JESSICA

This is so romantic. I feel like the girl in that story.

LORENZO

What girl?

JESSICA

The Verona girl. You know…what's her name?
You know the one. She married that young boy.
That's who we're like. Our families do not get

along, but we are passionate lovers too.
Just like them.

They kiss.

LORENZO

Juliet?

JESSICA

Yes, that's her. Juliet. Pretty like me?

LORENZO

Not pretty, my love…Beautiful like you.

JESSICA

What was the boy's name? I forgot his name.
Juliet's love?

LORENZO

Yes, the boy she married.

JESSICA

I'm not sure. Ruben? No, I think it was Roderigo.

LORENZO

Not Roderigo. Rome? No, not it…O,
I remember. Romero. Yes, that's it.

JESSICA

That's it, Romero and Juliet. That's
who we are like. Young lovers just like them.

LORENZO

But, Jess, didn't they die in the story?

JESSICA

Oh. Yes. I think they died... because of love.

LORENZO

That won't be us. Let's choose another couple.

JESSICA

How about Cleopatra?

LORENZO

And I would be Caesar?

JESSICA

No, silly, the young one.

LORENZO

Mark Antony?

JESSICA

Yes, that one. He was a Roman hero.
A great hero. She was his lovely queen.

LORENZO

I like that. That's who we are.

JESSICA

And he didn't die.

LORENZO

Wait, she died. It was a very bad death.

JESSICA

How did she die?

LORENZO

Uh. Uh. Snake bite, I think.

JESSICA

Snake bite?

LORENZO

In a bad place.

JESSICA

Where? On the Nile?
Near the desert sand? In a pyramid?

LORENZO

No. Where mothers suckle their young babies.

JESSICA

Let's not use them as a guide to romance.

LORENZO

We could be like Troilus and Cressida?

JESSICA

Lorenzo, let us be the heroes of
Our own story. Let's write our own chapter.

LORENZO

Yes, let's write a new chapter as lovers.
We start in secret, then pull off the covers.

They kiss.

Black Out.

Scene 3

OTHELLO enters Shylock's home stage left. Old Gobbo greets him.

OLD GOBBO

As salamu 'a laykum.

OTHELLO

Alaykumu as-salam.

OLD GOBBO

Come, Master Shylock is in his workshop.
Dost thou care for refreshment, Othello?

OTHELLO

Yes, friend, tea would satisfy, my dry throat.

OLD GOBBO

Chinese tea? I'll make it a priority.

Old Gobbo crosses to stage right followed by Othello. Lights up on Shylock carving a majestic wooden chair. It is ornate and beautiful. He has on a carpenter's apron, and there are wood-carving tools at his feet. Shylock has been working on the right arm of the chair.

SHYLOCK

Greetings (he rises and kisses each cheek). I see you have weathered the storm.

OTHELLO

The Cyprus storm withers not. War goes on.
My duty's done, yet more is often asked.
Christians give me a pain. Impolite, false,
and rude. They want me to dance to their tune.
Then pat me on the head as a reward.

SHYLOCK

We live in one of the most progressive
cities in the world, yet I must deal with
the tiny minds of bubble mouthing men.

OTHELLO

What is this carpentry that you do?

SHYLOCK

A secret. I trust you so you must keep
my indulgences silent, Blackamoor.

OTHELLO

As I trust you.

Othello examines the work. He looks at the right arm of the chair.

OTHELLO

A woman's face you carve with grace and care.

SHYLOCK

My wife's face. She was strength, my right arm.
Now her image will stay with me as long
as this chair stands. And I was going to carve
my daughter's face on this chair's left arm, but
she has disappointed me. Now I think
I will carve the face of an angry dog.

OTHELLO

But why a dog?

SHYLOCK

That bitch has hurt my heart.
I think I have lost my daughter. I send
one of my tribe, Tubal, to ferret out
information. If he be a true friend
He'll advise and counsel. I trust him too.

OTHELLO

I'm sure Jessica will be found, my friend.

Shylock looks at the carving on the chair.

SHYLOCK

She has her mother's eyes. O my Leah.
I loved Leah beyond all measure. She
wasn't just my wife, she was my being.
The oar that guided my swift gondola.
The earth that nourished my poor Hebrew roots.
The sun that lit my darkest charcoal moods…
Jessica has her eyes. Her mother's fire.
And she delights in life's simplicity
If her mind's made up, it's a mind unbent.

OTHELLO

And why?

SHYLOCK

Because she has her mother's eyes.

OTHELLO

I have no child, can offer no counsel.

SHYLOCK

Enough of me, share with me your news.

OTHELLO

I'm a warrior, Shylock, and I have
lost my right arm, a stellar soldier.
Would that I could carve his face on a chair.

SHYLOCK

And who might this brave comrade soldier be?

OTHELLO

My lieutenant Fabrizio, stellar!
I mourn Fabrizio Iannucci.

SHYLOCK

The hazards of war, my friend Othello.

OTHELLO

Now I have soldiers clamoring for his
seat. Lesser soldiers desire reward.

SHYLOCK

Crabs in a barrel, making that hard climb.

OTHELLO

To add an insult to his memory,
I'm asked to aid in domestic chores which
Thrill me not. Politics always bore me.
Yet I am called on to sup at the tit
of a pompous Venetian Senator.
At his urging, our pestiferous Duke
insists my sweet humble soul pander to
Venice motley-minded ivory elite

So I sup with Brabantio tonight.
A trite evening that will be. Friend Shylock,
It is so good to see you once again.

SHYLOCK
   Othello, let that gentile dine alone.
Let us break bread, let us solve the problems
of the world. Our eyes see the same vistas.
We sit in the same chair as immigrants.

OTHELLO
We can talk world politics, but I must
save my appetite. Thy servant offered
the refreshment of Chinese tea for me.

SHYLOCK
I will eat with you. I will drink with you.
Will not you do the same with me, my friend?

OTHELLO
I swore my stomach to this Venetian.
Let us enjoy the time 'till I must leave.

Old Gobbo enters with tea. Shylock examines the tea.

SHYLOCK
Old Gobbo, what tea is this?

GOBBO
'Tis oolong.

SHYLOCK
Old Gobbo, my belly quivers tonight,
Bring Moroccan mint tea for me, it sooths.

Old Gobbo nods and hands Othello a cup of tea and exits. Shylock takes off his carpenter's apron.

OTHELLO

No wine for you?

SHYLOCK

I join my guest in tea.
As your host. I remain sober of mind.

OTHELLO

And how is the news on the Rialto?
How fare you in finance? All debts repaid?

SHYLOCK

These Christians don't practice their religion.
Debtors who refuse to pay debts or want
to trump the bill. O, 'tis a huge disgrace.

OTHELLO

My debt is this visit's prime occasion.

He hands Shylock a bag of gold.

OTHELLO

Paid in full.

SHYLOCK

'Tis all here?

OTHELLO

Yes.

SHYLOCK

I know this.
I will count it anyway, Othello.
I'm nothing, if not a mathematician.

OTHELLO

Shylock, you are an honest man, for sure.
Ne'er say that the Moor is not honest too.

SHYLOCK

Even so. Why can't Christians be like us?
             Othello, we understand each other.
I am a Jew, thee a black Moslem, Moor.
We have a respect for each other's skills.
We do not try to cheat, abuse, or lie.
You need gold, I lend you my gold. Simple.
So a contract is made. Agreed upon.
Then, you, my friend, satisfy the contract.

OTHELLO

Si, I am a man of my word, Shylock.

SHYLOCK

Prago…But this Goy is a true liar.
Anything to get the upper hand.
This white reptilian will rewrite my
history, anything to keep the Jew
in the shade of lies. These Italians have
taken one of my heroes and claimed him
as a Christian.

OTHELLO

And what hero is this?

SHYLOCK

Black Moor, have you visited Firenza?
The Palazzo Della Signoria?

OTHELLO

No. Before the war is over, I will.

SHYLOCK

This Michelangelo Bounarotti
Carved a beautiful Carraran marble
statue of our Hebrew hero, David.
The statue is exquisite. Majestic,
The anatomy takes your breath away.

OTHELLO

He is a genius. I see no problem.

SHYLOCK

The problem is his penis, not Jewish.

OTHELLO

You mean…

SHYLOCK

Yes, David is not circumcised.

OTHELLO

That's odd. Very odd, Michelangelo
a brilliant artist. He would know of this,
The Moor would know more, infantile error.

SHYLOCK

The church. They hate Jews so much they would take
our hero and make him theirs, not ours.
They rewrite our history and create lies.

I must use the reputation white men
have created for the Jew, maximized
to advantage. I'd be a fool not to.
Am I ignorant of their righteous hate?
and ignorant of their covetous greed?
Am I ignorant of their disdain for
the original Jews. Let them suck up
to Jesus, then denigrate his people.
Let them draw Jesus to their breast, then in
his sacred name desecrate his people.
Let them cry to the heavens as they sink
into their own hollow-eyed Christian hell.
This duplicitous gentile. Uses fear
of us to further his control on their
Venetians peasants. So I become their
whipping dog. Their cur that must learn to heel.

Old Gobbo returns with Shylock's cup of tea. He serves as they talk.

SHYLOCK
I took a great risk. You might not return.
This Cyprus war rages with assured death.

OTHELLO
I took a greater risk. My life hanging
in the balance. Bad news for me, if I die.

SHYLOCK
For you and me both. Othello, thou art
a noble beast. You made sure you would live,
live, so thee could repay the Jew thy debt.

OTHELLO

Ha! O, I have other reasons to live.
We're outsiders trying to stay level
in a city that floats, an unbalanced world.

SHYLOCK

My tribe is at a slight disadvantage.
A consequence of being Nomadic.

OTHELLO

Yes, but they can see me coming, my friend.
There is no hiding black skin on white silk.

SHYLOCK

Black skin, red hat, and white Factious Gentiles
find a way to separate us, always
They point evil heinous fingers with glee.
Here behind these Ghetto walls must I live.
Walls with Christian gates they openly lock,
disposable like caged animals.
I see a barren spirit in their eyes.
Yet if they prick us, think'st we will not bleed?
and if they tickle us will we not laugh?
So if they poison us, will we live on?
They think they disgrace me by making me
wear this red hat, 'tis my badge of honor.

OTHELLO

Forget to wear that red hat, who will know?
Jew, Christian, you all look alike to me.
I can never hide, ebony skin for
it shines brightest at noon as the orb rises.

Shylock has finished counting the gold and takes a sip of tea.

SHYLOCK

Ah, there 'tis. All here, my sepia friend.
Whether 'tis nobler in purse to suffer
slings and arrows of contagious ill will
or to take lame ducats against troubles
and by borrowing seeming to end them.

Shylock bites the coin to make sure it is real.

OTHELLO

Jew, so how could you doubt this big black Moor?
A whiff of garlic? Do I Christian smell?

SHYLOCK

I doubt not, my friend, but not every man
                    is as forthright as you, proud Othello.
I have a loan made to a Venetian.
Antonio, I suspect he will not
honor his bond. O, 'tis so sad, but true.

OTHELLO

Then why make the loan? Seems nonsensical.

SHYLOCK

I know, but I hate him. He's called me cur,
and spit upon my splendid gabardine,
I decided to add a caveat.
Can't repay, the Jew, give a pound of flesh.
There are no gentle gentiles, I have found.

OTHELLO

A pound of flesh?

SHYLOCK

Weight of the human heart.

OTHELLO

And he agreed?

SHYLOCK

He's a moron. Who knew?
I have no intention on collecting
his bond this way, but I need insurance
to renege would be foolish. So foolish.

OTHELLO

Shylock, you should be more trusting, my friend.
Antonio, his debt will he repay.
These Venetians seem to be simple folks.
Look for treachery, Jew, you will find it.

SHYLOCK

Zounds, Ne mo me impune laccessit.
"No one provokes me without punishment."
Keep up your guard, Moor. If you relax, these
Italians will try to take advantage.

OTHELLO

Jew, you amuse me. You forget white men
are simple animals. Look in their eye,
he will tell you who he is. Eyes don't lie,
Lend him mercy, not gold. Lend compassion.
Not thy precious time, O, save that for us.
Save your money for us who will need it.
We fight the same foe, yet live divided.
He will be honest and repay thy debt.

Shylock, I find thy tea satisfying,
our company, witty and jocular,
but the time has come for my departure.

SHYLOCK

Take care, Othello, beware false Christians
You are naïve, Moor. Thou art a leader,
O, but you are no negotiator.
The eyes will always lie. Just takes practice.

OTHELLO

I go to sup and dine Christian cuisine
to tell stories and share all that I've seen.

Othello exits. Old Gobbo collects the glasses as he exits. Shylock looks after his friend.

Black Out.

Scene 4

Lorenzo and Jessica are at the altar. They are getting married. They have wedding rings on their fingers.

PRIEST (Voice Over)
You may now kiss the bride.

Lorenzo lifts her veil and kisses Jessica. She breaks the kiss and whispers in Lorenzo's ear.

JESSICA
Where is the glass?

LORENZO
What glass, Jessica?

JESSICA
The glass you break, we all yell, "Mazel Tov!"

LORENZO
Jessica, no glass is broken in church.

JESSICA
But 'tis a wedding tradition. 'Tis good
luck for the married couple to break glass.

LORENZO
Not in a Christian church.

JESSICA

Lorenzo, if
we don't do this, t'will be bad luck. I'm not
superstitious…but with the blending of
our lives, we can't afford any bad luck.
Can't we break the glass?

LORENZO

No, I would like thee
to accept traditions of our religion.
Thou art a holy Roman Catholic now.

JESSICA

No, yelling Mazel Tov, either, my love?

LORENZO

No, Mazel Tov either. 'Tis your new life.

JESSICA

Before I leave my old life, would you do
your bride one favor. Would'st thou stomp thy right
foot and whisper in my ear, Mazel Tov.

Lorenzo looks at Jessica gives her a quick peck and stomps his right foot then…

LORENZO (yells)

Mazel Tov!

Jessica hugs him.

Black Out.

310

ACT III

Scene 1

Othello enters Shylock's home.

SHYLOCK
How now, Moor. (He kisses each cheek) Relax, let us share our thoughts.

OTHELLO
Jew, I need a friendly ear.

SHYLOCK
Black man look
No further. Shall we drink and talk, shall
we break bread. I am at your disposal.

OTHELLO
No drink today. May I bend thy ear, friend?

SHYLOCK
I shall imbibe, for my stomach has woes.

Shylock pours one goblet of wine. Othello shakes his head no.

SHYLOCK
Have these gentiles caused you grief in your life?

OTHELLO

I have woes that have creeped into my world,
but also the promise of a great joy.

SHYLOCK

An ear for troubles, a heart for great joys.

He raises his glass to toast Othello and sips.

OTHELLO

Thy stomach?

SHYLOCK

Steady as an empty pail.
I too have woes, so after we have solved
your problems, you may lend an ear for mine.

OTHELLO

Good council for each, and friend supports friend.
How many women think you I have had?

SHYLOCK

You're a soldier, more than I know, less than
you'll admit. You have found love. I can tell.

OTHELLO

You can tell? Marriage is in my future.

SHYLOCK

You are contemplating giving up your
freedom for love. On marriage, the first thing
a man does is count his legacy and
well, on his past 'ere looks to his future.

Shylock takes another sip of wine.

SHYLOCK

I think this wine be past its prime. Taste it.

Shylock offers the glass to Othello and Othello declines.

OTHELLO

I believe you. I need not verify.

SHYLOCK

Old Gobbo! I pray come hither, Gobbo.

OTHELLO

Friend, I've fallen in love.

SHYLOCK

Is this woman white?
Or found you a woman of Islamic faith?

OTHELLO

Her name, Desdemona, and I love her.

SHYLOCK

Will she convert to Islam?

OTHELLO

I think not.

Old Gobbo enters.

OLD GOBBO

Master Shylock, I'm here at thy request.

SHYLOCK

Here, take this vinegar that masquerades
as wine. Gobbo, bring me a fresh bottle.

OLD GOBBO

Red or white?

SHYLOCK

A bottle of red, of course.

Old Gobbo exits.

SHYLOCK

And so, you trust this Venetian woman?

OTHELLO

I didn't say trust. I said love, Shylock.

SHYLOCK

So thee would give up Allah for marriage?
Abandon your religion, say not so?
For a Christian woman, ye hardly know?

OTHELLO

Not uncommon. Many men before me
Have fallen in love and so trusted their
instincts and passions they felt for true love.

SHYLOCK

But her religion…you're converting to
Christianity. These priests, my black friend
are deceitful men. T'will use you for their
personal gain, in the name of their God.
I am a Jew. I do business every

day with Gentiles, but rather do business
thee, not some foot licker of bunion toes.

OTHELLO

I lead Catholic white men on the field of
battle, I know their hearts, Think'st it easy
to inspire killing? Think again, my friend.

SHYLOCK

       Yes, you are their general, Othello.
Christians don't follow their own religion.
They are led by the nose from priests that tell
them very little, use them mightily.
You understand Jehovah is Allah.
They fight over the messenger and not
the ultimate goal. Adam and Eve is
in the Torah, the Bible, and Qu'ran.
Cain, Abel, or Avraham and his sons.
If we all worship one God, our tongues call
him different names, yet tell me, why must we
fight? They accuse Jews of killing Jesus,
it benefits them to do so. Sinners
disguised as saints, look only for profit.

OTHELLO

I am not marrying the religion.
I am wedding Desdemona, Shylock.
She is a good Christian. What care I if
there be bad Christians? There be bad Moslems.
Every creed has its villains. Why should I
then, not find happiness in my lifetime?
This ivory Queen brings me absolute joy.

Old Gobbo returns with a fresh bottle of wine and pours it in front of Shylock.

SHYLOCK

Thou think'st you're walking into a love match.
Desdemona says she loves you, therefore
to marry her, you must convert. Simple…
but there are consequences to this act.
Gobbo, 'tis better bottle, tasty.
Will Allah curse your ebony soul, Moor?
Will this Christian religion fail you, Moor?

OTHELLO

Shylock, you forget one important thing,
I've found something I have always wanted.
I ask, when you married, sir, t'was it love?

Old Gobbo hands the fresh glass of wine to Shylock. Shylock raises his glass to the memory of his wife.

SHYLOCK

O, my Leah was my heart's sacred dream.
I drink to her mem'ry. Thanks, Old Gobbo.

Old Gobbo nods and exits.

OTHELLO

So please, think on the joy your wife brought you.
Please think on the birth of your Jessica.

SHYLOCK

O, please do not mention my daughter's name.

OTHELLO

Is Desdemona my heart? 'Tis so true

Christianity is but a little
price for a Moslem to embrace his joy.

SHYLOCK

I have woes that only a child can bring.

OTHELLO

You are rich. What woes do you carry that
cannot be solved with gold? 'Tis Jessica?

SHYLOCK

My daughter! O, my daughter!

OTHELLO

Is she dead?

SHYLOCK

Aye, to me. She has been corrupted, Moor.
Stolen away from me and abused by
Christian cunning. There is a gentile named
Lorenzo that wants to marry my child.

OTHELLO

Is he a good man?

SHYLOCK

Moor, he's a white schmuck.
Not of my faith. He will turn my lovely
flower into a weed. I do not want
my Jessica to become a Christian.

OTHELLO

Shylock, I now consider the same fate.
I now see your resolution and your
determination so to confine me.

SHYLOCK

How can I now lose two dear people to
the same demon? O, 'tis too much to bear.
Do you think I would give up all I know
to embrace a religion whose source comes
from Jews? Jesus was a Jew, a rabbi.
These Christians love Jesus yet hate all Jews.
Gentiles look to us and say we killed Christ,
as if we nailed that Hebrew to the cross.
The Romans are not seen as complicit.
The weight of Jesus and his crucifix
is the sole burden of my Hebrew tribe.
These priests influence other Gentiles with
lies and intimidation to spit on
Jewish gabardine and think us villains
and money-grubbing fools. 'Tis a sad plight.
They will go to war, fight with races of
other countries, conquer them, rape them, and
steal all that they own. Let thirty years pass
and all is forgiven. But for my tribe?
Fifteen hundred years cannot erase their
Jewish hatred, these Gentiles know how to
hold a grudge and build resentment on it.
How do succeeding generations hate
with such passion? You think I can come to
Venice and own land? Nay. Can I come to
Venice and apprentice a trade, be a
carpenter or a wheelwright? They say nay.
I love carving chestnut, oak, beech, poplar.
But these goyum pass laws that forbid it.
Jews are given two choices. Make clothes or
lend money. What if I have a talent as a
Silversmith, a wheelwright? No, not for a Jew.
I must wear this red hat so that Christians
unsure of my heritage will know to

treat me as less than human in Venice.
They will kiss a dog in the mouth and let
the cur drink from their cup ere they will show
a Jew, Christian humanity. 'Tis so.
Now my Jessica wants to embrace the
very people that cause us Jews dark woes.
Worse, she wants to marry one. My foe she
joins in matrimony, 'gainst my wishes.
My enemy, our enemy, and her
reason? She thinks she loves this Lorenzo.
The only thing we Jews have in this world
is faith. Let him come to Judaism.
Let him convert. Let's circumcise, the dog.

OTHELLO

Shylock, I can see I have arrived at
a time when you must needs have solitude,
so I will give it you. I must be gone.

SHYLOCK

Please hear me, Moor. Heed the words I have said,
Best die on the floor than a Christian bed.

Black Out.

Scene 2

Shylock is moaning and holding his stomach. Old Gobbo holds his hand. Guinevere enters.

GUINEVERE

You called, Father?

OLD GOBBO

Guinevere, where is your
Brother Lancelot? Call him here for me.

GUINEVERE

Gone. Running errands for Bassanio.

OLD GOBBO

Gone? Find me Shylock's doctor.

GUINEVERE

No problem.

OLD GOBBO

Bring him here. Stomach pains overtake our lord.

Guinevere exits to find a doctor.

SHYLOCK

Old Gobbo, my daughter has married, fled,
and left me with pains, such pains in my heart.

OLD GOBBO

Soon. Her ghetto return is eminent.

SHYLOCK

Beware your children, Old Gobbo, beware.

OLD GOBBO

Raising a daughter can be difficult.

SHYLOCK

I need a doctor. This pain grows, Gobbo.

Shylock sits in a chair.

OLD GOBBO

Guinevere will not fail us. My daughter
Shall find the solution to your troubles.

SHYLOCK

Old Gobbo, my daughter has fled from me.
For what is a young man to do after
having been husband? What choices abound?
Why he looks to the day of his firstborn.
That penultimate day of his marriage
The day that erupts with a daughter's birth
and parenthood is the consummation
of divine family love. The patriarch
looks forward and then imagines all the
scenarios fatherhood can magnify.
From cradle to adulthood, thy child grows,
carefully parsing out the life lessons
you will share. Using your religion as
a guide post to success as she becomes
a lovely girl, strong woman, a lady.
Where thou had no patience, family gives birth

to this stranger, you shine the light of time
on this evasive subtle foreigner.
You welcome patience and strive to master
the art of parenting…what's your reward?
Your offspring steals from you. She takes from you.
Dips her hand in the well of security
and takes what is mine as if it were hers.
Let her save her own ducats and share those.
All my hard-earned past divided up to
a self-serving gentile…for what? For love?
She sees…yet ignores the truth of her eyes,
Venice hates Jews…and rather than bear the
weight of all her ancestors, rather than
observe Yom Kippur or our Passover,
she takes the easy way out. Rather than
learn to bend, she breaks with her past, she now
embraces this heathen Catholic land.
She becomes Christian. For Jehovah's sake…
A Vatican Catholic. My child grows
to adulthood and now abandons me,
It's as if she stood and saw the results
and decided she was not a fighter,
not a soldier. She saw our tribe's struggle
and decided, our struggle shamed her.
So she married a shagitz. Is't false love?
Christian love! Better she should stab me in
the heart with a crucifix. If Lorenzo
Loved her? Why…convert to Judaism.
Let him join the fight. Suffer as a Jew.
Instead, like some low-life cockroach, this Goy
entices my daughter to abandon
her family and steal away to Jesus.
O, children can bring you your greatest joy,
and make sure you feel your deepest sorrow.
I am sad, I am hurt. I'm fatherless,

for my child hates me and she knows not why?
She embraces the very thing that hates
us. She'll never be free, no matter how
far she travels they will always see who
she really is the truth of that cannot
be denied, in her heart, she is a Jew.

OLD GOBBO

I know 'tis not easy to raise a child
in this world. So many hard distractions.
So many pitfalls. We that aren't native
to this land must fall under the yoke of
Christian morals. My son, Lancelot I
do not fear for…but, Shylock, my daughter.
O, my daughter is subject to the dark
intense ire and lascivious glares of
Christian perversions. Using my Moslem
religion against me. As a crutch to
do guilt-free abominations on our
women. I teach my daughter signs to look
for, signs to avoid, how to assess, so
that when those white men want to compromise
her virtue or her dignity, she has
choices to alter her situation.
Guinevere's sharp mental chastity belt.
Never walk into a room you can't get
out of. Position yourself so that you
gain the benefit of an uneasy
situation. White men love their power.
They love flexing their muscle on weaker
souls not protecting the less fortunate.
They have no empathy nor care for us.
I try to give her life lessons that will
protect her and aid in her survival.

TED LANGE

SHYLOCK

Does she listen?

OLD GOBBO

There is a certain youthful arrogance,
Parent to child is a very hard road.
You try to remind them of lessons learned.

SHYLOCK

Your daughter steal from you?

OLD GOBBO

No. Of course not.

SHYLOCK

Jessica knows who I am. Who I love.
Where she comes from. Only your child can cut
through the tender part of a parent's heart,
seize it in her hands and punch you over
and over again till your insides bleed.
It is not a fair fight, when a gentile
can capture the only true thing you love
in this world and helps himself to her fruit.
Make sure young G holds tight thy heritage.

OLD GOBBO

Who can say, Master Shylock? I am sad
to see you in this mood and with this pain.

SHYLOCK

I am hurt…and the pain in this belly
of mine is not helping. So imagine
a Jew that hates being a Jew. Silly.
I love being a Jew. I love the fight.
I love being outnumbered by this pale

324

SHAKESPEARE OVER MY SHOULDER TRILOGY

foe. Then with wit, with guile, I outsmart 'em all.
Only a Jew can do that. I can look
in their eyes and see their ebonic hearts.
I love a good fight, a fair fight, but my
child hurts me, Old Gobbo, she hurts me.

*Guinevere enters with RODERIGO LOPEZ. He is carrying a wooden box
filled with vials.*

GUINEVERE
Your worship, I bring you Doctor Lopez.

SHYLOCK
Where is my doctor?

LOPEZ
Gone on a short trip.

SHYLOCK
Are you a Jew?

LOPEZ
What difference does that make?

SHYLOCK
You're not a Jew. I want my own doctor.
Gentile doctors, I don't trust. Never have.

LOPEZ
You're ill. 'Tis no matter, who brings the cure.

SHYLOCK
You could poison me. Antonio could
have arranged this. Guinevere, my doctor?

GUINEVERE

Travelling. He's set off for Padua.

SHYLOCK

Padua?

Shylock moans.

LOPEZ

Let me examine you. If you are not
satisfied with my diagnosis, fetch...

SHYLOCK

I know you not...What are your credentials?

LOPEZ

I am visiting from England. I am
only here for a few weeks. I was told
of your need. I took an oath to cherish
life, be it Hebrew, Moslem, or Christian.

SHYLOCK

Thou art in Venice, not England. Gentile
doctors can't minister to a sick Jew.
It's the law. I don't want your prognosis.

LOPEZ

Laws are meant to be bent. So in good faith
I can't walk away from suffering souls.

SHYLOCK

Don't walk away. Run! Goy, there is nothing
you can say to change my mind or move me.

LOPEZ

I see you must have verification
of my medicinal skills. I am a
member of the College of Physicians
and the Doctors Guild in England.

SHYLOCK

O, think not you that thy words impress me.

LOPEZ

As Doctor, I served the Earl of Leicester,
the Earl of Essex, and on occasion,
I most modestly admit I have been
Physician to England's Elisabeth

SHYLOCK

That bitch.

LOPEZ

Thou share some of her qualities.

SHYLOCK

Babble if you wish, I will endure this
pain, 'till a Hebrew doctor comes along.

LOPEZ

What brings you the most Joy?

SHYLOCK

What do I love?

LOPEZ

Yes. What gives you more pleasure as a man?

SHYLOCK

Since my Leah has passed, I find myself
carving wooden boxes. I like working
with my hands, yes, being a carpenter.

LOPEZ

A Jew that is a carpenter, hmmmm.
I will tell thee, friend, what gives me great joy.
Unlocking the secrets of nature. We
have mysteries at our fingertips.
'Tis an art to all medicine, my friend.
Like a craftsman's inclination to herbs,
that carry medicinal benefits,
yet have I a talent for finding what
works for the human body. I love the
challenge. I love solving the mystery
of the human spirit of a distrustful patient.
I took a solemn oath as a physician.
T'was Hippocratic. Thee challenges my
ethics. So I ponder, how may I use
my natural skills to repair thy body?
Make thee feel healthy. Bring thee back to thy
regularity. Thus, cure your disease.
I can think of but one thing to tell thee,
that might bring us a positive outcome.

*Lopez looks at Shylock for a beat. Looks into his eyes, then leans over to
Shylock's ear and whispers. Shylock reacts to what he hears. They lock eyes.*

SHYLOCK

Say that again…slowly.

Lopez takes a beat, smiles, then leans down again to Shylock's ear and whispers.

SHYLOCK

What is a reasonable man, if he
be not willing to try new doctor techniques.
I will let you examine me. I will
swallow pride and suspicion and put my
trust in you, Doctor Lopez, Venice tourist.

LOPEZ

And so, I thank you, kind sir, for your faith.

As Lopez checks Shylock, Old Gobbo signals Guinevere. They step aside and talk.

OLD GOBBO

As your father and his servant, I have
seen nothing like this.

GUINEVERE

Did I do all right?
Is this a worthy success?

OLD GOBBO

Yes, my child.
So where did you find this Doctor Lopez?

GUINEVERE

In Ghetto Vecchio. Master Shylock's
doctor had left the city and I asked
for a replacement and was directed
to this Doctor Lopez as capable.

OLD GOBBO

He has a sturdy persuasive manner.

LOPEZ

Guinevere, please boil me some water. I
would like to make an herbal tea with some
of my own ingredients. I think I
know what will be helpful to Shylock's pains.

Lopez opens his box. Takes out a vial, then follows Guinevere off stage.

OLD GOBBO

Are you satisfied my Master Shylock?

SHYLOCK

I trust him. Shall we see what comes of this?

OLD GOBBO

May I ask what Doctor Lopez whispered?

SHYLOCK

Gobbo, when a man whispers in your ear,
It is a secret. Shall this old Jew break
that covenant for gossip? O, I think not.
When he brings my tea, I hope it is hot.

Black Out.

End of ACT III

Intermission

ACT IV

Scene 1

Lorenzo and Jessica are on a ship.

LORENZO

Art thou fulfilled?

JESSICA

I now have a new life.
I have the love of you and of Jesus.
I revel in our new matrimony.

LORENZO

And thy conversion to being a Christian?
This pleases thee? Sweet Jesus, not soft regrets?

JESSICA

I embrace Jesus Christ. Was he not a Jew?

LORENZO

Si, Jessica…Now there are two Jews in
my life. I embraced both with unbounded
love, passion, and reverence. Please come close.

He kisses her.

JESSICA

Such tender lips. Such strong heartfelt passion.
I look to the day we soon bring new life

into this world. To bind my world with yours.
The day thou becomes a father will be
our day of great joy and of motherhood.

LORENZO

Lady J, I thought you unattainable,
a dream, kept apart my custom and our
Italian Christian prejudice. Hampered,
but God blessed me. I saw you and prayed for
guidance to thy Hebrew heart. I prayed hard.

JESSICA

Thy prayers were answered as I knelt to bring
you closer to me. I leave my Hebrew
teachings to gain a Christian education.

LORENZO

Together, we face this world united.
Venice society will try to fight it
The burden is heavy, we will lighten it.

Black Out.

Scene 2

Shylock is sitting in a chair, carving on a wooden box. Lopez enters.

LOPEZ

Feeling better?

SHYLOCK

You're a miracle worker.

LOPEZ

What work is that?

SHYLOCK

Wedding gift for the Moor.
What thinks thee of this Italian city?

LOPEZ

'Tis fascinating the power of herbs
and it grows here before us. It is the
reason for my journey to this country.
I hope to find the clear medicinal
benefits of Italian herbs, wild plants.
I'll take them back to England. It puts me
Ahead of my rivals. My garden in
London is the envy of most doctors.
Thus, if I have medicinal plants not
available to my contemporaries,
then my immediate value increases.

SHYLOCK

So, Doctor Roderigo Lopez, I am
Delighted to find out thou art a Jew.
Thou whispered in Hebrew, no less. You knew
I'd believe thee, how? Elucidate, friend.

LOPEZ

Your stomach pain aided all my options.

SHYLOCK

And I have a question for you. If Jews
were expelled from England in 1290,
how does a doctor escape notice of
English gentiles and royal privilege?

LOPEZ

O, we Jews are a resourceful people.

SHYLOCK

Some Jews. Not all Jews. Me and you. The rest
I can count on my left hand. How'd you do it?

LOPEZ

It's a story…but I don't want to bore.

SHYLOCK

Yes, bore me…Please, Doctor, sit and bore me.
I have bad family troubles that I must
not think on. Your story will distract me.

LOPEZ

If I take time to share my tale, I must
have complete secrecy.

SHYLOCK

We are brothers.
Thou art not talking to a gentile, friend.

LOPEZ

So swear on your life as an honest Jew.

SHYLOCK

By the words in my Torah. Your secret
will be kept…as Jehovah's the one true God.

LOPEZ

As you know in 1290, the English
decided enough of Matzah eaters.

SHYLOCK

Most Jews know of King Edward's edict of
expulsion. At least when you get to be
my age, you look for a welcoming face.

LOPEZ

Our history. Some of our youth are not
as informed as we ancient ones.

SHYLOCK

Sometimes, knowledge in youthful hands carries
no weight. If my child doesn't know England's
history…she knows of our fights in Venice.

LOPEZ

Shylock, I'm a Crypto-Jew.

SHYLOCK

A Marrano?

LOPEZ

Si. Mi padre, Antonio Lopes
was physician bto the king of Portugal.

SHYLOCK

King John III?

LOPEZ

Si. He converted for
the king and I was baptized into the
Holy Roman Catholic Church. But...
We secretly practiced our Hebrew faith.
There are a number of Marranos in
Portugal.

SHYLOCK

How do you find each other?

LOPEZ

Our last names. So as not to expose ourselves,
we changed the spelling of our surnames.
Any Christians with the letter Z in
their last name could be a Marrano.
L.O.P.E.S. becomes L.O.P.E.Z.
You direct the conversation, and we
will carefully reveal ourselves.

SHYLOCK

Are there still Marranos in Portugal?

LOPEZ

Yes, many.

SHYLOCK

If it is a secret, how does one Jew
find another?

LOPEZ

As you walk about London, if you see
a household with two candles side by side
that is a signal. Return on Passover
You will be rewarded and delighted.

SHYLOCK

Fascinating, Roderigo Lopez,
but why leave Portugal for English soil?

LOPEZ

I decided to seek my fortune in
England, and there are many Marranos
living here in the city of Venice.

SHYLOCK

There's no need to hide your Jewishness here.

LOPEZ

Shylock, some Jews don't want a ghetto life.

SHYLOCK

Cannaregio is a badge of honor.

LOPEZ

Some Jews hate the idea of reporting
to this evening ghetto and locking all
the gates, while gentiles are free to walk about.
Waiting till noon for the key, caged liked animals.

SHYLOCK

I've seen no Marranos here in Venice.

LOPEZ

Ever had a case tried in Venetian Court?

SHYLOCK

Si, of course, a number of cases. So?

LOPEZ

Did you win? 'Member the cases you won?

SHYLOCK

Si, I can count them all on my left hand.

LOPEZ

Those cases thou did win, those Judges were
Marranos. The system is set up for
Christians, not Jews. A Jew can never win
a lawsuit fairly with a Christian judge.
'Tis designed to look fair and impartial,
but every law bends away from we Jews.

SHYLOCK

Thou gives me now concern for my law suit.
Collecting on his debt lacked my purpose
it was insurance to fortify, but
Christians now take everything from me, so
time to pay the Jew his due. Look how they
treat us and abuse us, cheat us and lie.
Marranos hiding in plain sight. Doctors
hiding underground. 'Tis a sin, my friend.
I will never do that. I wear my faith
as a badge of honor. My red hat I
wear proudly. Let them see me coming.

I love the fight. I love beating the Goyim.
With wit and guile, they surrender purses
to me. Only a smart Jew can do that.
You're a Marrano, but that's not for me.

LOPEZ

Each soul travels his own path. My father
paved this road before me. I but try to
improve on the gifts he left for me.

SHYLOCK

You came at the right time for me. I was
in great pain. I'm cured. What did you give me?

LOPEZ

An herb. Aniseed. Potent and effective.

SHYLOCK

I feel better. I feel so much better.
May I suggest to you as a tourist,
you must visit The Castello. Campo
Santa Maria Formosa has a
beautiful open-air theatre.

LOPEZ

Everyone says that.

SHYLOCK

Two thousand Jews can't all be wrong.

LOPEZ

I will take my time and tour the city,
Seeing new sights, so Italian, so pretty.

Black Out.

Scene 3

Old Gobbo dresses Shylock as he goes to trial.

OLD GOBBO

So, Master Shylock, you wear your best gabardine?

SHYLOCK

Yes, Old Gobbo, I will not have them see
me in nothing less than my very best.
Those Goys wish to laugh at this ol' Jew, but
I will give 'em pause. They'll know this trial is
not about ducats, 'tis about justice.

OLD GOBBO

Yes, sir, it is. Will your daughter be there?

SHYLOCK

O, my Jessica has forsaken me.
She renounces one thousand years today.
She sets aside all she was raised to be,
to shame and show spite for me. I ask but
one thing from her, be a loving Jewess.
We are immigrants, to every country.
All countries in the world show us contempt.
Must I give my past to forge my future?
No, say I. A Jew, I wear that title with honor.
This country may hate an immigrant, yet
beg for our services. I relent for

I am a good Jew. An honest Jew.
A man of scruples and integrity.
Yet my Shayna Maidel betrays her past.
Oh, my daughter breaks my heart and spits on
all that she was taught to be. 'Tis a sad
day, Old Gobbo, I raised a faithless Jew.

OLD GOBBO

Hark, your heart.

SHYLOCK

Old Gobbo, leave me.

Old Gobbo exits as Jessica enters and finds her father dressing.

JESSICA

Papa!

SHYLOCK

Here daughter.

JESSICA

I ask you not to go to trial today.

SHYLOCK

Again, you break my heart, little Princess.

JESSICA

Papa, why are you going through with this?

SHYLOCK

For my bond. Princess, I finally got 'em.
Their weakness, the law. Bends to my service.

JESSICA

A pound of flesh? A harsh bond to collect.

SHYLOCK

And by law, they must satisfy my suit.

JESSICA

Papa, don't do this. Be the better man.
Listen to your bright forgiving angels.

SHYLOCK

I can't believe thou art here now to
advocate for that Catholic goyish scum.

JESSICA

Papa, please, I am now a new Christian.

SHYLOCK

Stop please, Jessica, I taught thee better.
Thou gives up our heritage, our history
and your noble heart to this white man?
You disgrace me. You of our struggle.
We immigrants fight for our survival...
without a second thought, thou giv'st all to
Lorenzo. This Italian gigolo?

JESSICA

Papa! He's my husband.

SHYLOCK

Hater of Jews.

JESSICA

Not all Jews, he loves me.

SHYLOCK

Or your money.
He marries not a Jew. You convert and
He marries a freshly minted Christian.

JESSICA

We're in love…can't you be happy for me?

SHYLOCK

How can I be happy for you? I lost
my daughter and gained a dark enemy.
He took you away from your Hebrew past.
To the point, you think thy father 'tis thy
enemy and thy enemy your lover.
Thy husband stripped you. Extinguished thy fire.
Replaced it with doubt, circumspection, and
self-loathing. Art thou an anti-Semitic Jew?
Thou hast walked away from the crusade for
A Catholic! A white man! A Pork swilling…

JESSICA

Just stop it! I can do it no longer.

SHYLOCK

Can't do what?

JESSICA

Be a Jew. I can't fight this
war you love. I feel more Italian than
Jewish. I can't stand what being foreign
means here. I want my freedom on this land.
I'm done making sure I come back to this
Ghetto, locked in to free the Goys. Show up
or we will lock you out and leave you to

the mercy of the city. Better to
be a Christian in a Catholic city,
surrounded by other Catholics. Papa,
'tis the same God, Allah, Jehovah we
worship. Jesus was a Jew. I am a
Jew for Jesus.

SHYLOCK

Daughter, we are not family.
Be gone from my sight. Do not infect my
eyes. Jessica you are now dead to me.
No wife, no child, alas, no family.

Jessica starts to say something, Shylock turns his back on her. She exits.

SHYLOCK

I take account of this trial. I have loaned
Antonio three thousand ducats, which
he gave to Bassinio. What purpose
I know not? Nor care not. With a promise
to return my loan he failed, knowing that
my bond would be a pound of his flesh.
Now we must go to court to ensure the
bond is paid. I know these Christians will try
to forfeit payment. But I'm in the right.
What ere my intention, a man without
his family has nothing left to lose.
So with or without a Marrano judge,
I stand on truth and justice for a Jew,
Yes, Antonio, I know he hates me,
spits on me, calls me low-life dirty cur.
This is my revenge, for all Jews that he
has consistently wronged. I can see no
other outcome but success. I puzzle,

why do Christians always ask victims
to be the bigger man as they rape us.
I know the law, it cannot be broken.
This pound of flesh is just a bloody token.

Black Out.

Scene 4

Old Gobbo and Guinevere in Old Gobbo's home.

GUINEVERE

A man from China asked me about the Shylock trial.

OLD GOBBO

What did he ask you?

GUINEVERE

Why are Catholics so angry with all Jews?

OLD GOBBO

What did you answer?

GUINEVERE

I had no answer.

OLD GOBBO

Daughter, what do you mean by no answer?

GUINEVERE

Shylock goes to trial, demands his pound of
flesh. The Christians refuse. This yellow man
wants to know why is this so important?

OLD GOBBO

Yes. These religions are really angry
with each other.

GUINEVERE

Why?

OLD GOBBO

Each believes that as
far as Allah is concerned, they're both right.

GUINEVERE

Papa, how can that be? No, both are right?
Do they think one is closer to Allah?

OLD GOBBO

We are Moslem, but we're not strict Moslems.
As you know I don't pray nearly as much
as I should. Jews and Christians discount us.

GUINEVERE

Why such anger with Christians over Jews?
Both hold the Ten Commandments as sacred.

OLD GOBBO

As does Islam. This yellow man has asked
a profound question, insightful and wise.

GUINEVERE

He is a philosopher, my Father.

OLD GOBBO

If we all believe in the Allah of
Avraham, why is there such derision?

GUINEVERE

Yes. Why? Papa, can you explain, simply?

OLD GOBBO

I gather my thoughts; I'll try to explain.
Not an easy task. Let me see. Let's see,
Ah yes, picture this, there is a mountain.

GUINEVERE

Mount Sinai?

OLD GOBBO

Good as any. Let us say
Allah is at the top. There are three tribes.
Jews, Catholics, and us. Each strives for the top.
So we pick a trail. Jews have their trail up
the mountain, Catholics have another trail,
Islam has a third choice. Each tribe follows
their path, and at the end of a lifetime,
you follow the sacred laws to the top.

GUINEVERE

One mountain. Three trails. Three names for Allah.

OLD GOBBO

Yes. Allah, God, and Jehovah. We all
worship the same Deity but use a
different name. Same stories in the Qu'ran,
are shared in the Bible and the Torah.

GUINEVERE

Adam and Eve?

OLD GOBBO

Yes.

GUINEVERE

Noah and the Ark?

OLD GOBBO

Certainly. My daughter. Yes, all the same.

GUINEVERE

Moses on the mountain with the tablets?

OLD GOBBO

Absolutely. Guinevere, it's the same.

GUINEVERE

So why do we all fight? We believe in
the same Allah. Isn't Allah happy
that we all worship him? Thou shalt have no
other Allah before me? So why does
Shylock demand a pound of flesh? Why would
Antonio take him to court? If they
want justice and they share the same God.
Wouldn't they show mercy to each other?

OLD GOBBO

So many questions, little girl. Maybe
we should ask a priest or ask a rabbi.

GUINEVERE

I could ask the Chinese philosopher.

OLD GOBBO

Guinevere, let your father explain with
another example. O let me see.

GUINEVERE

As your patient daughter, I will listen.

OLD GOBBO

Now, let me see. Three books, yes, let me see.
Qu'ran, Holy Bible, Torah, each sacred.
Each book's telling the same story differs,
Yet has details special for that reader.

GUINEVERE

I am lost in this holy example.

OLD GOBBO

Think of it as three cookbooks. A fine meal.
Let's say we need a recipe for chicken.

GUINEVERE

Chicken?

OLD GOBBO

Yes, chicken. Let us say the Jews
were the first to discover that bird is
Delicious and edible. So they roast
the chicken. They plucked the feathers, devised
a spit, prayed as they slowly turn the bird,
so, the chicken would be cooked on all sides.
Rabbi writes this recipe in his book.
They passed the book around and told other
Jews how to cook chicken. Another cook,
Says he is a chef. He cooks chicken too,
Differently. Don't roast it, bake it. Jesus
is this new chef. Twelve Jews like his cooking.
The twelve join Jesus for their last supper.
He's refined the recipe, the menu.

Older Jews predict a new cook might come
along, when they tasted Jesus's chicken
they said "We're sticking to our Recipe.
We don't like the way his chicken tasted."
A third chef comes along with another
new recipe who is our Mohammad.
He tastes both dishes and he says, "I have
a better way of cooking this sacred bird."
He offers his own newer recipe.
He decides to slowly stew the chicken.
Every chef asks his flock to pray over
the meal. Be grateful and Allah, God, and
Jehovah will bless you and bless the meal.

GUINEVERE
Then why fight? It's still chicken, isn't it?

OLD GOBBO
Exactly. But each religion has its
own cookbook, each religion thinks their book,
the one true light to an excellent meal.
My feeling is…we should all be able
to dine at the same table, praise Allah,
and enjoy the meal. There are those that will
not allow you to eat unless you feast
off of their menu. Eat their meal or fight.

GUINEVERE
Allah has provided a hearty meal.

OLD GOBBO
It all goes in and it will all come out.
When Allah is with you…be a better person.

GUINEVERE

Yes.

OLD GOBBO

So have you learned your lesson for the day?

GUINEVERE

Yes, Namaste, my Papa, Namaste.

Black Out.

ACT V

Scene 1

Jessica talks to Lorenzo about her Shylock.

JESSICA

I worry for my father. I worry
for his life. I pray suicide is not
harbored in his mind. He can hold a grudge.

LORENZO

Your father's anger in losing this case?

JESSICA

For sure. Did you notice anything odd
about the attorney that argued the case?

LORENZO

Antonio's lawyer? What durst infer?

JESSICA

I found Antonio's lawyer oddly queer.
Did you not see that? Or maybe felt that?

LORENZO

I'm at a loss for the text of your meaning.

JESSICA

I thought his lawyer strongly feminine.

LORENZO
Jessica, thou think'st him, lover of men?

JESSICA
A lover of men? Why yes. I think so.

LORENZO
I say no…Maybe a little effete.

JESSICA
Small hands, wide hips, and slow gait. He seemed to
me more like a brilliant she. Smart and sharp.

LORENZO
Jessica! You're being ridiculous.
You' don't like fops. So you think he's a fop.

JESSICA
You misunderstand. The quality of
mercy was a stroke of genius, genius!
I just thought he seemed a little softer,
as a person. Strong words, soft demeanor.
Maybe an educated hermaphrodite?

LORENZO
I had no such misgivings. I thought him
to be an exceptional debater.
Smart, well-spoken, and very masculine.
His knowledge of the law? Impeccable.
Beyond reproach. Antonio did well
in choosing him to represents his interests.
So Shylock loses and Antonio wins.
Who cares if his attorney is a puff.
Certainly Antonio doesn't care.

maybe you are carrying anger 'cause
your father was beaten…beaten fairly.

JESSICA

Look at his losses. He must give thee half
his fortune. Convert to being Christian.

LORENZO

His conversion to Christ won't go easy.
Agreed, first he must sign over the deed
to his wealth, his property. All is shared.

JESSICA

If he were not such a stubborn man full
Of Judaism and ducats. He sought
Justice in the wrong house. A sense of right
and wrong as if he dealt with Talmudic
scholars. A Christian white man looks at his
justice with a different set of cold eyes.
Had he thought better, his mercy should have
dropped as a gentle rain. Then he would have
been twice blest. He'd stayed a Jew. Stayed solvent.

LORENZO

Jess, your father's loss now becomes our gain.
From Jew to Christian, you'll never be the same.

Black Out.

Scene 2

Othello enters Shylock's home as Shylock loads a chest with sacks of money. There is a bottle of wine on a small table. Occasionally, Shylock's sips a glass of wine.

OTHELLO

Shylock, look at me. Do I look different?

SHYLOCK

No. Black as yesterday, black as 'morrow.

OTHELLO

Islam black or Christian black? Tell me, Jew?

SHYLOCK

Say it isn't so? No, Moor, not Christian.

OTHELLO

Why dost thou stare? Yes! I convert for love.
I hear thou art a Christian too, my friend.

SHYLOCK

Not willingly. I lost my pound of flesh.
Lost my three thousand ducats, lost my faith.
'Tis a sad day for this daughterless Jew.

OTHELLO

I thought you came willingly to Jesus?

SHYLOCK

Antonio! For shame that canker sore.
That pustule of oozing carbuncle.
He trapped me with clever Venetian law.

OTHELLO

How is this true? Shylock, how is this true?

SHYLOCK

O, you know what these Christians said to me?
The quality of mercy is not strained.
Mercy not strained? As if they have mercy…
Or practiced mercy. Shall I list my battles?
Of the crusades? Shall I list the moments
In history when their eye became blind
To the sights of pillaging, raping, or
murder and the cries of their enemies
called for "mercy." Shall I talk about
this Cyprus war that you are now fighting?
But they say to me, it droppeth as the
gentle rain from heaven upon the place
beneath. Angry rain from hell I say.
Twice blessed? Oh, yes. Blessed for me and blessed
for them. So do I get my pound of flesh?
Do I get my justice? Do these Christians
see the fairness of my bond? Hardly so.

OTHELLO

You lost your case! No justice and no peace?
So why is it that you pack? A small trip?

SHYLOCK

'Tis a secret, Moor. My own private secret.

OTHELLO

What was your judgment?

SHYLOCK

Yes, I could cut off
his flesh, but shed no blood. Nor cut less
nor cut more than a pound. Do not achieve
this I risked my life. My bond turned against me.

OTHELLO

Friend Shylock, what was the end result?

SHYLOCK

My enemy Antonio insisted
to the judge I become a Christian and
relinquish half my wealth to my Jessica
and her Lorenzo...or die. I should die.
Die? Zounds, why, die I? Where's my fucking mercy?
So where is my twice-blessed Christian goodness?
For when a Jew looks to his oppressor
the laws serves him not. Unless he turn Christian.

OTHELLO

Hard to be a Jew in a Christian court.

SHYLOCK

Split half my fortune for Antonio
half for the state on pain of death, big O,
On pain of death. My friend, on pain of death!

OTHELLO

It did not go well.

SHYLOCK

I tell you, Black man,
these Christians are duplicitous devils.
The fatal straw, Antonio will not
make me forfeit my wealth if I enter
the Christian door and convert to his faith.

OTHELLO

So you did?

SHYLOCK

What choice have I? Death or Jesus.
To prove my conversion, they set a plate
of pork before me and demanded I eat.

OTHELLO

Not good. I was put to no such test.

SHYLOCK

You went willingly to this heathen faith.

OTHELLO

I support you; we can worship as friends.

SHYLOCK

Infamy. If thou think this Jew will toss
away his faith, then you don't know Hebrews.

OTHELLO

Ex-Jew, did thou not give your vow to God?

SHYLOCK

And presently I sign this deed, so that
All my wealth goes to my daughter's husband.
Another knife twist from Antonio.

Oh, Othello, I am undone. I am
branded a Christian and must now survive.

OTHELLO
I have happily converted for the
Christian pathway to Allah. So Amen.

SHYLOCK
I say amen in a pig's eye, Big O.

OTHELLO
I do not feel as you feel, friend Shylock.
I shall embrace this Christian religion.
It brought me my future wife and lover.

SHYLOCK
When will thou marry?

OTHELLO
'Tis so, tomorrow night.
That's my secret that I entrust to thee.

SHYLOCK
Are you sure this is the woman for you?

OTHELLO
There comes a time in a man's life when he
takes stock of his past and looks to progeny
and what footprint he will leave in his lifetime.
I am a warrior. I know battles
I have won. I have fought well for this white
man and was well paid. But now I want the
spoils of my career, so what does he prize
above all? His woman, I cared not for
his taste 'till I met young Desdemona.

Here's a prize above all other prizes.
This woman with skin of alabaster
captured my heart. I am like a child
again wanting to please her. I like this
feeling. She asks for my faith in Jesus,
I give it gladly. She asks for my hard
adventures, I gladly share them. I am
pleased that in this year of my life only
by accident has Allah blessed me with
The lovely virginal Desdemona.

SHYLOCK

I wish thee all the best, Moor, with this new
chapter in your life. Here's a gift for thee.

Shylock goes to a shelf and gets an intricately carved wooden box. He gives it to Othello.

SHYLOCK

For thy wedding night.

OTHELLO

I thank thee for this gem.

SHYLOCK

Now, I ask you Moor, does her father know?
Have you her father's blessing for marriage?

OTHELLO

No, friend Shylock. 'Tis a secret to him.

SHYLOCK

Moor, I will tell you this, as a man who
lost his daughter to deception, tell him.

OTHELLO

Christianized Jew, I ask you, tell me this?
Had Lorenzo come to you, with request
for Jessica's hand, would'st thou given it?

SHYLOCK

Never.

OTHELLO

Your pearl, Jessica, you'd throw away?

SHYLOCK

Yes, away. Base Judean as I am.

OTHELLO

So what makes thee think Brabantio would
be more forgiving than you, friend Shylock?

SHYLOCK

Othello, what makes you cry?

OTHELLO

Cry? I am a soldier. A warrior.

SHYLOCK

You never shed a tear?

OTHELLO

To cry or not
to cry, is that the question?

SHYLOCK

Thou art a brave man, but in your travels,
Thou hast seen things that brought tears to thy eyes?
Something that peeled away the clouds around

your heart, that center cavity in your
soul, that connects to your brain…so when you
least expected, ocean floods your dark eyes?

OTHELLO

Shylock, hang your tears out to dry.
There have been moments in my life I know
that should have overtaken my emotions.
Think you, many forms of death paraded
before me. The many times I've stood in
battle and witnessed triumph and defeat.
Think thee a moment would reveal itself
to me. But no, no tears, no sorrow, none.
Would Homer cry? Would Jason stand before
his Argonauts and weep? O, I think not.
In point of fact, I've trained myself not to
let tides wash onto the shores of my cheeks.

SHYLOCK

I hate deception, Ex-Moslem, I do,
But I see your point. I wish you the best.
I hope that when Brabantio finds you
to be his son-in-law, he'll embrace you.

OTHELLO

I think her father loves me, but I do
not want to leave my life to chance or luck.
Let it be a certainty. Desdemona
and I will welcome the bright aftermath.

SHYLOCK

Blessings on you both.

OTHELLO

Come, my friend, witness
my nuptials. Come tomorrow night and
be a part of my new life and wedding.

SHYLOCK

I'll away Moor, late, I will let it be
A white bride, a dark mate wedded shall I see
I'll watch thee become a husband and gain a wife.
May it be the happiest day of your new Christian life.

Othello shakes his hand and leaves.

Black Out.

Scene 3

In Lorenzo's house, Guinevere is waiting for Jessica. It is nighttime.

GUINEVERE

In this chest is Shylock's gold and his jewels.
The wealth of this country amazes me.
Citizens work hard to just earn enough
to sustain themselves…yet there are those that
would tax, steal, swindle what little peasants
earn to line purses. Banks manipulate
the rules to benefit the White elite.
Those societal pigs run this country
on a lie, and we immigrants aid and
abet the lie 'cause it is worse to live
anywhere else in modern Italy.
Christians say they will be tolerant of
other creeds, yet if thou art not Christian…
Thou wilt experience difficulty
finding equality. So this Jew goes
To trial to fight for his equality,
set up under their justice and their laws,
alas, he's not a Christian. He's a Jew.
He looks like a Jew, smells like a Jew and
most importantly acts like a mad Jew.
He has been given few options in this
foreign land. The elites have ensured his
demise specifically designed for
his downfall. Anytime they want to try

and implement control or tighten their
grip on a non-Christian they are allowed
to do so. Shylock believes in the pure
natural superiority of
his Hebrew mind over the Christian way
of doing things. If these lowlife bastards
played fair, he would have won. The wealth of this
country is controlled by elite Christians.
Rule of law will twist and bend to ensure
control over Moslems, Jews, the peasants
and any immigrant that sets foot on
this soil seeking a better way of life.
We immigrants don't mind working harder.
Don't mind suffering through a dark day to
enjoy the bright moonlight of the evening.
Our body is safe and sound. Our family
thrives as we're taken out of harm's way to
face less danger…but a price is hard paid.
Colossal wealth of this country surely
amazes me. The cake is baked, and so
the elite slice off a nice big piece for
themselves, leaving the crumbs for the rest of
us to share, and we…accept it. Stale cake!
Not many of us get to eat cake…but
if you have a taste for it, make sure you
are not a Jew. Be a Goddamn Christian.
In the trial, Shylock was sentenced to
give up his wealth to his Christian offspring.
No pound of flesh for this Jew. And for his
audacity in opposing white men,
his gold was taken away. His freedom
to remain a Jew abolished on pain
of death. His only child, now converted,
must share Shylock's profits with a Christian
husband. This country's wealth amazes me.

It sits in the white hands of the elite,
under the guise of their Christian fairness.
Dive thoughts deep into my black Islamic
soul. Here comes the fresh newly Christian wife
Jess with benefactor mate Lorenzo.

Jessica and Lorenzo enter.

GUINEVERE

This is the last chest.

JESSICA

You've had a long day.

LORENZO

Guinevere, thank you for all your help. This
money is an unexpected windfall.

GUINEVERE

Shylock fills his legal obligations.

JESSICA

I know this pains my father.

GUINEVERE

Very deep.

JESSICA

I know we are both daughters. We both have
feelings for our fathers. Your Padre is
a much more reasonable man than mine.
I sometimes look at you and your father
and wonder what in my padre angers
me so. I have no answer...I have no...

LORENZO

Jess, please…

JESSICA

No, husband…my Father, he should
be celebrating our marriage instead
he stews in a dark sour mood. He rails
against Jehovah and calls me traitor.
Expects more than less.

GUINEVERE

Your padre…is…now…

JESSICA

Yes. Spit it out, Guinevere. Please do not
stutter or stammer or bite your pink tongue.
You are free to speak your mind. 'Tis a free…

GUINEVERE

No. I must go.

JESSICA

I see thoughts that betray dark eyes. You can speak to me freely.

GUINEVERE

I must go…

Guinevere exits.

LORENZO

Strange girl.

JESSICA

'Tis so unlike her.
What is she hiding?

LORENZO

Who knows what beats in
this child of Hagar's heart? Secrets abound.

Guinevere re-enters.

GUINEVERE

Mistress, I must speak to thee. I cannot
hold my thoughts inside. My dark thoughts linger.

JESSICA

Speak, Guinevere, speak. Share your thoughts with us...

GUINEVERE

I was sworn to secrecy...but I feel
as a daughter, I must share this pain or
I would never forgive myself, if I
let this time pass and you were ignorant
of thy father's dilemma.

JESSICA

Say no more.
I understand...He hates being Christian.

GUINEVERE

More than that...the ultimate step to end
degradation and Ashkenazi pain.

JESSICA

Ultimate?

GUINEVERE

Si, he has poisoned himself.
He is dying, mistress. His time is short,
he has but now a few hours to live.

JESSICA

Say 'tis not true. Tell me a different tale.

GUINEVERE

Oh, yes. After the trial and during his
conversion…he loathed himself and he took
Mandragora, to ease his mind and kill
his body. Or maybe we think it was
Hyoscyamus niger, both poisons
very deadly. Only his Hebrew soul
and spirit waits for his last redemption.

JESSICA

Lorenzo, come we must comfort Father.

LORENZO

Oxymoron. Comfort Shylock. We know,
Impossible, Jessica, but we go!

JESSICA

My Father takes poison to ease his pain.
His spiritual exit, my golden gain.

Black Out.

Scene 4

*Shylock is on his death bed. Lights up on Shylock is in his bed as Jessica lis-
tens. Old Gobbo is close by as is Guinevere. Lights up slowly as Lorenzo is in
the middle of his speech to his father-in-law.*

LORENZO

Am I a lucky Christian? 'Course I am.
My family knows it. My friends all know it,
I know it. Even you know it, Shylock.
Every once in a while, my God smiles down
on a hapless soul and fills his wish list.
Did I know it would be your Jessica?
Of course not. I thought it would be some young
blonde Italian girl from a noble family.
Northern girl. Did I think for one minute
my heart would be captured in the Ghetto?
So like the iron works that once sat here,
would I find my love too, built on iron?
A foundation forged within these high walls.
Shylock, I love Jessica, more than you
know, and my final wish to you is that
regardless of our differences, you may
open your dark eyes and see my true heart's
admiration and compassion for Jess.
Like the bloom of the *Cyclamen* I grow
then blossom as a man every day I
share my life with her. Like the scent of the
Quercus suber tree, I breathe air of dreams

fragrant of Jessica, alive with us.
I will honor my wife 'till my last breath.
I will endeavor to seek a union
built on trust and affection in marriage.

SHYLOCK

Trust, affection, and Christianity.

LORENZO

Yes, she has left her faith, but I assure
you my faith and religion will comfort
her spirit and her precise timeless soul.

SHYLOCK

O, young Goy, every child you conceive will
be a Jew. The race of the child comes from
his mother. Conversion or not, such is
our custom. I pray you tell your little
Lorenzo, Grandpa Shylock was a Jew.

LORENZO

Jew in race, Christian in soul. May they come
to Jesus Christ is my ultimate goal.

SHYLOCK

I'm going to be sicker than I am.

LORENZO

I will leave you to spend time privately
with my wife, your Jessica, our true heart.

SHYLOCK

Take her with you, she is now dead to me.

JESSICA
No, Papa! Know that although we differ...
I still love you.

SHYLOCK
You think you still love me.

Lorenzo exits.

JESSICA
We can love and disagree. It is the
right of every daughter to see life through
her own eyes. Papa, I do not deserve
this animus you have for my new life.

SHYLOCK
I raised you differently. I raised a Jew.

JESSICA
And now thou art a Christian. Where's the love
expressed in the heart of the Torah? So
where is the do unto others, Papa?

SHYLOCK
Through trial and error, I must arrive here.

JESSICA
I pray for your recovery. I know
God is merciful, he will bring you back
to your new family. I share all my gains
with you. All blessings I will share with you.

SHYLOCK
Jessica, let me die in peace. Let me
please leave this world as I came into it.

Hold no service for me. Let me pass as
I ordained in my will. Old Gobbo has
instructions. I am weak…This is the last
time I shall see you. I am too weak to
resist this Christian nation. I die soon
a loathed gentile, never to worship
in a synagogue again. Never to
pray to my Jehovah. Aye, me. Life has
its final laugh on me. Girl, leave me now.
I am too weak to carry on, too weak.

JESSICA

Papa, I'll pray for your immortal soul.

SHYLOCK

Jessica, my time is here. I just want
to die well. I do not want to whimper
or cry for this world. I want to face death
and cross over as a man. I hope I
will be a prime example of a man
with a belief in Jehovah that can
face his own death unafraid. I need a
true stepping-stone to the unknown, daughter.
A man to face his quiet end alone.
Now, leave me to my own thoughts and my prayers.

Jessica kisses him on the forehead and leaves.

SHYLOCK

Call the doctor. I feel myself going.
I don't want to leave without him knowing.

Black Out.

Scene 5

Shylock sighs as Doctor Lopez pulls a vial out of his case. He hands it to Shylock. Old Gobbo is packing clothes into a trunk. Shylock sits in the majestic chair. It is the finished product of his carving skills.

LOPEZ

Another sip.

Shylock drinks the liquid.

SHYLOCK

Tastes bitter.

LOPEZ

Yet it works.
Shylock ,thou will feel thy strength soon return.

SHYLOCK

I am tormented by the vows I gave
these Christians when I adopted this new
religion. Will my soul be newly damned?

LOPEZ

Kol Nidre will protect your soul, my friend.

SHYLOCK

Are we aligned? Will our English plan work?

LOPEZ
Si. All is prepared for your arrival.

SHYLOCK
Lopez, I thank you for your assistance.

LOPEZ
Have you said your familia goodbyes?

SHYLOCK
I am done. Only Gobbo knows our plans.

OLD GOBBO
A question, Master Shylock, what is this
Kol Nidre? Please enlighten this poor soul.

LOPEZ
We Jews take a solemn vow against vows.

SHYLOCK
Old Gobbo, every Yom Kippur we face
the future with Kol Nidre prayers, indeed.
From the Day of Atonement, we all pray.

LOPEZ
It allows us not to be held hostage…
by our previous vows. It releases
us from all the vows we were forced to make
or lies we had to embrace to survive.
Prohibitions, oaths, consecrations, vows that
we may vow swear, consecrate, or upon ourselves
prohibit. So now we add Yom Kippur.

SHYLOCK

From Yom Kippur until next Yom Kippur,
may it come upon us regarding them
all we regret them henceforth.

LOPEZ

They will all be permitted, abandoned,
cancelled, null and void, without power and
without standing.

SHYLOCK

Old Gobbo, our vows shall not be valid vows;
our prohibitions shall not be valid
prohibitions and our oaths shall not be
valid oaths.

OLD GOBBO

'Tis a wonderment, Yes? Master Shylock,
every religion fascinates me so.
But my work. Your fresh adventure awaits.
I shall procure servants to deliver
this old trunk for your new travels abroad.

Old Gobbo exits.

LOPEZ

I have here three letters of introduction
once you reach London. Guard these carefully.
If they should fall into the wrong hands, the
lives of three Crypto-Jews are in peril.
They will of course assist you with a new
identity. Shylock dies here tonight.
But the Phoenix will soon rise in England.
You must now live there as a Christian man ...
but you will soon be free to practice your

religion in secret. You will join our
Hebrew fraternity. I will return
to England in seven months. I will be
there to help you with any needs that arise.

SHYLOCK

Life's new adventure begins as I use
my wits to overcome my enemies.
Doctor Lopez, my one true love is wood
carpentry. I will be able to carve
and ply my trade. I will use my hands on
oak, beech, maple wood and know that I can
make a living following my true dream.
I leave being a broker of ducats,
knowing wood carving must now sustain me.

LOPEZ

Will you carve chairs like the one that seats you?

SHYLOCK

Chairs, tables, wooden boxes. Anything
made of wood. I want to be known as the
new Michelangelo of wood carving.

LOPEZ

When asked, be sure to tell these Englishmen
you come from Firenza, with that accent.
No need for foreign eyes to look to Venice.

Shylock starts to cry.

SHYLOCK

A new life. A new role and a new world
for me to conquer. An old man finds a
new chance at life with his God Jehovah.

LOPEZ
Why do you cry, old man? Why do you cry?

SHYLOCK
I weep for all the possibilities.

LOPEZ
Tears of joy or sadness?

SHYLOCK
I'm no longer a Jew, I am a man.
No preconceived prejudices meeting a man.
I will rise or fall now on who I am
Not what they've heard from friends. Dark rumors of
hatred won't fill their hearts. Their minds will
be clean and unsoiled. I can greet a
stranger as a stranger myself, not a
strange Jew. I'll stand before an Englishman
as his equal. Not less than, not more than.
We can discover our likes and dislikes,
Not shaded with corrupt passions of thoughts.
Head to head, toe to toe, equals. I now
            understand my friend Othello, I truly
see his dilemma. No matter where he
travels, he arrives as a black man first.
Foreigners see color before the man.
Can he ever see the truth of their hearts
in their eyes? I stand on the threshold as
a new Shylock. I can open my heart
not as a Jew, but as a man. When a
man hates me, it will be for the truth of
who I am as a man. Not his dislikes
for a race of people. My life as a
Jew stands as a shadow in the night. This

is a new day for this old soul. Bless you,
Roderigo Lopez, you have opened my heart
to vast infinite possibilities.
Better to be an immigrant Goy than
a travelling Jew.

LOPEZ

A future London bright.
You'll sing English songs of love and delight.
Travel to England, become a new man.
Still a Jew in a foreign land.
When your ship docks in England's London Bay,
Then recite the words of our Kol Nidre.

Shylock gives himself the Catholic sign of crossing his body.

LOPEZ

Ve'esarei, Ush'vuel, Vacharamei, Vekonamei, Vekinusei, Vechinuyei.

LOPEZ / SHYLOCK

D'indarna, Ud'ishtabana, Ud'acharimna, Ud'assarna Al nafshatana.

Lights up on Jessica and Lorenzo, Stage right, they are kneeling and praying in a Catholic church, they kneel before a Catholic cross. Lights starts to fade center stage on Lopez and Shylock.

LOPEZ/SHYLOCK

Miyom kippurim zeh, ad Yom kippurim Habba aleinu letovah.

Lights up on Guinevere stage left. In a room, she has a wooden carved box. She takes coins out of the box and is counting her money. She is making notations in a small notebook. Lights up on Othello, upstage right. He rolls up his prayer rug, then places a crucifix around his neck. He turns and kneels facing the same cross that Jessica and Lorenzo pray to. They are all praying to a Christian God. Lights up on Old Gobbo, up stage left, as he kneels on a

prayer rug and prays to Allah. Stage center; underneath the fading light is a single spotlight on Shylock's face.
As the stage lights dims center stage on Lopez, the spotlight on Shylock face seems to burn bright.

LOPEZ/ SHYLOCK
Bechulhon icharatna vehon, kulhon yehon sharan.

Lopez now stands in darkness as a shadow, his voice is silent. Only Shylock can be heard finishing the prayer, the spotlight shines brighter on his face.

SHYLOCK
Sh'vikin sh'vitin, betelin umevutalin, lo sheririn v'lo kayamin.

Lights go to black on Jessica and Lorenzo, Guinevere, Old Gobbo, and Othello.

SHYLOCK
Nidrana lo nidrei, V'essarana lo essarei
Ush'vuatana lo shevuot.

*Shylock is smiling now into the light. The lights hold for three beats…then…
Black Out.*

END OF PLAY

CPSIA information can be obtained
at www.ICGtesting.com
Printed in the USA
FSHW010505250821
84296FS